Charlene Doak-Gebauer

DIGITAL SEXUAL VICTIMS: TRUE CASES

Parents and Caregivers
Learn how to protect your children
Learn about
DIGITAL SUPERVISION

CHARLENE DOAK-GEBAUER,

NNCP, RHN, B.Ed. (Bus.),
Hon. Bus. Specialist, Special Education,
Computer Science, Network Management

Tellwell Talent
www.tellwell.ca

ISBN
978-1-77302-120-1 (Paperback)
978-1-77302-119-5 (eBook)

Table of Contents

FOREWARD

"I have known Charlene Doak-Gebauer all of her life. Charlene's successful teaching career was interrupted horribly by an incident that led to her second career - that of advocacy for young people to whom the Internet, cell phones, and social media have become second nature. And therein lies the problem.

Many of the parents of these young people, along with their teachers, religious leaders, and well-meaning adults do not have any idea how to protect these young people from the myriad of dangers lurking on those devices that we now take so much for granted.

Charlene has made it her life's mission to do something about this. She began by setting up a charity, and speaking to as many groups as she could, but just could not reach the number of people she desired to reach. She set up a web site - www.childpornographyhurts.com, which allowed her to reach many more, but there were still too many children being victimized, to the point that they were lost into child prostitution, slavery, drug addiction, and ultimately for many, suicide. The book "Digital Sexual Victims" is the result.

Charlene has developed and copyrighted a theory called "DIGITAL SUPERVISION", wherein she outlines what parents, teachers and any interested adult could do to help young people (boys and girls) avoid the many thousands who troll the Internet, looking to take advantage of unsuspecting children. To say that this is a book that should be in the hands of every Parent, Teacher, Peace Officer and Library, is surely an understatement! We must first Educate ourselves, before we can help

Children all over the World who might fall victim to these predators. And they live, unknown-for now-in our midst!

READ THIS BOOK! Buy a copy for friends or for your local library. Help put an end to one of the greatest crimes of our century. Your children are much safer playing in a neighbourhood park, than they are when exploring and sharing on the Internet! One "selfie", taken by a naive young girl of her body, could be spread millions of times in just a few days! Our childhoods were so easy in comparison.

Thank you for writing this, Charlene. Even one life saved will have made it worthwhile. I predict thousands!!"

Dr. Gary R. Munn, B.A., B.Ed., M.Ed., PhD.

ENDORSEMENTS

"I began my teaching career in 1950. At that time, a black and white television was produced and only wealthy families could purchase one. Parents depended on the school system to educate their children. Both 'school and public libraries' were sources where one could gain 'knowledge' about the world, or choose books to read for 'pleasure'. Families worked together in the evenings doing household chores. Conversations amongst family members were common at mealtime. Board games were often played after supper or on weekends. These types of family interaction, fostered activities, which helped to teach children communication skills and build relationships. The world was considered a safe place at that time.

Today, news from around the world can be viewed within 60 seconds. Since the change of the century, computers, iPads, cell phones and digital devices have become mainstream. The digital age has mushroomed since the year 2000 and major changes have come about within today's society. Both parents in over 60% of families now work outside the home.

What Charlene Doak-Gebauer has developed as Digital Supervision is a theory that parents and professionals need to learn. Traditional parenting methods as experienced before the change of the century must now be expanded to include supervision of children while they are using digital devices. Charlene's book, "Digital Sexual Victims", has information invaluable to all adults for the much-needed supervision of today's children. The content in her book is a must read for all adults to ensure the safety of all of our children. "

ALISON PEARCE, B.A., B.ED., M.ED., L.R.A.M.
Educator and Author

Teacher, Special Education Consultant, Principal, Trustee
Toronto, Ontario

"This book offers a timely guide to the dangers lurking on the Internet and to children now subjected to a growing barrage of pornographic imagery and seduction by sexual predators. The author's extensive knowledge and grasp of technological advances provide an invaluable resource underscoring the urgent need for more vigilance in our own homes. It should be widely read and consulted by parents, teachers, law enforcement personnel, health advocates and policy makers."

ROSE A. DYSON ED.D.
Consultant in Media Education
Author: MIND ABUSE Media Violence in an Information Age

"It's evident that Charlene knows what she's talking about when she speaks about the cyber crime of child pornography. Her conviction to battle this modern monster is clear and she has calmly and confidently increased her arsenal. Charlene describes child pornography as a fairly new crime that's simply mushroomed, but that is also an accurate description of her personal crusade to arm parents, educators and concerned adults with the information they need to protect their children from those who would seek to harm them using their social media posts against them. This book is a first line of defense for anyone who cares for, or about, a young person using today's technology."

JENNIFER VANDERMEER, JOURNALIST

"'Digital Sexual Victims' has information that is helpful for parents, educators and anyone working with children. A must read. The history of the family that has been victimized emphasizes to any reader how vulnerable we all are to digital crime, anywhere in the world."

HEATHER THANE
International Educational Consultant, Author.

"We sometimes refer to the pre-Internet years as "the good old days". This is more than a little naïve, of course. Risks to children's safety and wellbeing were everywhere: traffic, disease, the school bully, the stranger in the park. Back then, we could more clearly anticipate, identify, see - and perhaps most importantly, teach children about- the risks or threats. Because of the almost breathtaking growth of the Internet, its ease of access, and its anonymity, we can no longer be surprised or ignorant about the corresponding rise in the numbers of cyber-criminals: pedophiles, pornographers, trolls, and predators. We teach children how to safely navigate traffic to get to and from school. Charlene's book helps to ensure that children can more safely navigate their way in cyberspace- so that they can clearly "see" the threat, as we did in "the good old days"."

LESLIE GRAHAM
OCT, B.A.(honours)., B.Ed.

DEDICATION PAGE

This book is dedicated to my wonderful family, and most importantly, little M. I love you sweetheart.

Some names have been changed to protect the innocent. The story about Jennie is in third person for this purpose.

Thank you to:

My husband, Mike, for his patience and support throughout the writing of this book.

James Williams, child pornography victim, for his contributions to this book.

Detective Constable Jeremy Spence, for his support and advice.

CHAPTER 1

INTRODUCTION

Most people use the Internet, social media, digital devices, computers, etc. on a daily basis. We are communicating electronically like never before in history. However, we also need to be aware of the negative channels within these communication possibilities. This book has been written to help everyone realize that child protection needs to be expanded to include digital supervision of all children.

This being said, parents, caregivers, professionals and guardians need to understand that children and youth making poor choices and putting themselves in detrimental situations digitally are in epidemic proportions. We cannot be bystanders any longer. The unwitting actions of our children and youth can contribute to the crime of child pornography. Child pornography is proliferating at a rate that is unprecedented.

The crime of child pornography has existed for many years. There are stories from ancient Greece and Rome, which have narrated the sexual abuse of children, with drawings as illustrations. Unfortunately, child pornography was not recognized as a crime until 1977. In the United States:

Protection of Children Against Sexual Exploitation Act – 1977 - the first federal law to ban the for-profit production and distribution of child pornography.

The Child Protection Act -1984 criminalized the activity of non-profit child pornography trafficking.

1986 – Realization that child pornography had long-lasting effects on children.

1990 - it became illegal to be in possession of child pornography.

1999 - international investigations of child pornography began.

2015 – all states had laws against distribution, and possession of child pornography, either for profit or not-for-profit. (U.S. Department of Justice)

July 23, 2002 - In Canada, the offence of accessing child pornography was added to the Criminal Code.

July 20, 2005 - Bill C-2 was amended. Inclusion of mandatory minimum penalties; and the definition of child pornography included written and audio materials. The full Canadian Criminal Code legislation related to the crime of child pornography is in Appendix A of this book.

It is becoming more common to hear newscasts about child pornography. People are realizing that the challenges of the victims of child pornography are perpetuated. Often, we read that predators receive what we perceive to be light sentences. We may not hear information about the unfortunate victims, nor is there follow-up. It needs to be understood that often the court decides to have a publication ban in order to protect the identity of the victim. Sometimes the name of the predator is not published for further protection of the victim. The victim has the right to have their name published if they wish, but in many cases, they do not. They want to avoid the social stigma that can develop in this type of victimization. For a child, the court will decide against publication because of the age. If there are light sentences, the Crown's hands may be tied because of legislation and case law.

How do the victims cope? They are victimized daily, knowing that predators are viewing their own abuse as they were recorded by picture or video. Many people believe this crime to be low on the statistics scale. Little do they realize that the crime of child pornography earns over $3 billion annually. These are the known cases of child pornography, for which there have been arrests of predators. There are far more atrocities that are not discovered, some of which are shared without income to the predators that are recording and sharing the pictures. Many share the pictures and videos without caring if they are earning an income from them. Others may not be defined as "pedophiles". They are engaging in sexually abusing children using cameras and video equipment as a means of creating a source of income from their victims.

Unfortunately, the Internet has helped predators and pedophiles find each other easily. This ease in communication has helped to give them a sense of family. This sense of common ground or "family" has helped to affirm their idea that assaulting children and youth is acceptable in an attempt to "normalize" their disturbing behaviour. They have a sense of "acceptance" within their twisted world. Victims are assaulted when the pictures/videos are recorded. The assaults are repeated every time the pictures or videos are accessed and viewed by other predators. This type of trauma is life-long.

In this book, you will learn more about the crime of child pornography, its effects on children and families, and ways to help parents, caregivers, and professionals help children and youth in making appropriate decisions for healthy and safe online usage and behaviour. The situations given are all true. I have developed a theory of "digital supervision©" which encompasses information required for adults to recognize online crimes against children, the proliferation of it, and the necessity for reconceptualizing child protection methods in this digital world. Digital Supervision is defined as a new branch of traditional parenting that includes digital guidance and supervision of children and youth.

"Everyday, I wonder what pervert is viewing my pictures. I was four years old when it happened. I will always be tortured by it."

— CHILD PORNOGRAPHY VICTIM

PART ONE

TRUE CASES AND CHARITY HISTORIES

CHAPTER 2

JENNIE

There are many situations involving the victimization of children using computers, digital devices and the Internet. Unless a person is a victim, or a predator has victimized a family, the effect of these crimes is difficult to comprehend. The general population believes that these crimes are horrid. They have little understanding of the magnitude of the proliferation of the crime and its effects. The story in the initial chapters about Jennie and her family will introduce readers to the magnitude of the effects of being victimized by digital crime. Jennie was just four when the crime against her took her and her family into a very nightmarish existence.

Since the 1990's, the digital age has matured and digital crime has become more prevalent. Parents, caregivers, and professionals need to comprehend the magnitude of the need to practice digital supervision for all children on all devices. Children, as young as four, are playing online games and being victimized by child predators who, while pretending to be a child, enjoy playing the games with the children, hiding behind a mask of anonymity. This story emphasizes the type of abuse that can be perpetrated by a predator who runs a for-profit or a not-for-profit child pornography business using digital devices. Too often, the predator is a person the child has been assured can be trusted, and, unfortunately, a person the parents trust. Always be alert to anyone who could potentially be a predator. A predator could be one or both parents, grandparents, aunt, uncle, family, friends, babysitters and on it goes.

Digital cameras were used in this crime, as well as computer equipment. The data was used in the digital child pornography industry over the Internet, as well as standard post. Read this story and come to realize the magnitude of the effects of this crime on the victim, the parents, and the entire family.

Play time...

"Hi Mom! Guess what? Nancy's Mom says I am so beautiful I could be in movies! Isn't that neat? Nancy said she wants to be in movies too!" Jennie came bouncing home from playing with Nancy across the street. She was so happy.

"Awe, sweetheart, I am so glad. I think you are beautiful too." Elaine responded to her daughter, Jennie, as she always does, with positive energy.

Jennie was so excited and so was Elaine. Jennie finally had friends. She looked exceptional in her blue velvet dress, lace around the collar, white ankle socks and black Mary Jane leather shoes. She had wanted to get all dressed up today to go to Nancy's. She said that Nancy's mother was pleased she had dressed up to play. She couldn't believe how beautiful Jennie looked.

Elaine was fatigued. They had just moved again and she was having difficulty with all of the changes for all four of her children.

They had moved from a home in another subdivision. Their old neighbours weren't really friendly, and they needed a change. Her husband, Doug, had built this house and they were very pleased with it. The layout was excellent with an open concept and all new appliances. Their lot was larger and in a section of the subdivision that was more private than in their other neighbourhood. The whole family was very happy there.

And so the story goes...

Jennie was four years of age, and was the third child of four in the family. She always struggled to have friends. It seemed wherever the family lived, there were very few children her age. Her older siblings were five years older and, at her age of four, her two-year-old brother was just developing and not at her level of maturity for a playmate. They were close, but this closeness would grow later as her brother matured.

Jennie would play with Nancy, four years old as well, just about every day. Many times her mother would call over to Nancy's house to ask that Jennie return home. Nancy's house could be seen from the front window of their home; it was diagonally across the street. Sometimes, it would take about 30 minutes before Jennie would come home after her mother called. Because this has happened with all of her children, Elaine was accepting of the time lapse. Children are often in the middle of a game or play and then come home. She was so pleased for Jennie that she usually never called a second time for her to return.

As time progressed, Jennie's parents noticed some subtle changes in their little girl. She seemed to be distant and non-communicative. They would wake her up in the morning and she would be irritable and never really talk directly with anyone in the house. This was puzzling because she was always a child who would speak her mind and talk about how things needed to be "fair" between her and her siblings.

Her parents were becoming quite concerned about their little girl, even though she had a friend in the neighbourhood. The distance in their relationship was growing and it hurt them deeply. All of their children were usually very happy, loving, and responsive to all requests. Jennie was beginning to be quite a challenge.

One day, Jennie came home and stated that Nancy's mother was a better mother because she didn't work like Jennie's mother. Nancy's mother had told her that earlier in the day. Elaine was shocked and angry. She explained to Jennie that many mothers work. Elaine worked in an administrative role and had a position of responsibility.

Elaine explained, "Look at all of our friends – they all have mothers who work. Your brother and sister have friends whose mothers work. It is quite common. That does not mean that a working mother is not a good mother." This became a difficult topic for Elaine because it was obvious that Nancy's mother had been saying things to Jennie that Elaine felt should not have been said. Elaine believed that no parent should discuss the parents of their children's friends in such a negative way. She really wondered what the reason would be for a parent to be so negative and cause a problem between a parent and a child.

Jennie's conversations and behaviours seemed far too mature for a four year old. The babysitter described a conversation she had with Jennie and Nancy while they were out for a walk near Nancy's house, that she found puzzling. Jennie had stated that she played with Nancy, using a stick that had an end that looked like the head of a dog. She further described that Nancy's parents had played the game with the girls. The sitter thought it seemed so unusual and had some personal ideas about what kind of stick it was. When the sitter told Jennie's mother about it and her thoughts, Elaine was concerned.

The next day, she called over and asked that Jennie be sent home from playing at Nancy's house. Nancy's mother said she would send her home soon. Elaine insisted that Jennie be sent home immediately. It still took 15 minutes for Jennie to return. Elaine began to wonder even more what was going on when Jennie was playing at Nancy's. She decided to make sure that every time she called to have Jennie sent home, she would insist that it be immediately.

Elaine talked to her sister, Beth, about the recent events and she said she hoped it was probably just a child experimenting with her body. Beth said it is seemed common with children and that nothing should be disturbing about it at all, but to keep an eye on it. Elaine was not convinced, but decided that she would just monitor the situation and see what might come of it later. She knew innocent experimenting could happen, but she had a mother's instinct that it just didn't seem right.

One day, Jennie was outside with her older sister, Judy. They were laughing and giggling. Jennie would jump over Judy and Judy would try to catch her. It was hard to figure out which one was winning.

Elaine and Doug were thrilled to hear that Jennie was playing so nicely with her siblings. Their hearts ached for her because she just didn't seem to fit in at times. It started after they had moved into the neighbourhood, but they still couldn't put their finger on what might be the trigger.

All of a sudden, Jennie stopped laughing, and yelled at Judy, "Show me your privates." She started dancing around Judy yelling, "Show me your privates, show me your privates, show me your privates! Right now!" Judy was very disturbed by it and just stared at Jennie in shock.

Judy went running into the house and told the sitter what had happened. She said Jennie was acting weird and told her to show her privates. The sitter was quite concerned and said she would tell Elaine. Jennie got very angry and went running upstairs.

Doug and Elaine looked at each other in bewilderment. Elaine went running upstairs after Jennie. When Elaine went into Jennie's room, she saw Jennie, sitting in the dark, looking out the window toward Nancy's house. Jennie said, "I wish Nancy's mother was mine – she lets us do whatever we want. She doesn't work either."

When the sitter told them, Elaine was devastated and tried desperately not to cry. She told Jennie that it was not a nice thing to say and to stop it. Her mother and father love her dearly and that is all that matters. There are certain things you should never do and telling your sister to show her privates is wrong. Elaine asked Jennie where she got that idea. Jennie said, "nowhere," turned her head to the wall and stopped talking. Elaine quietly left the room. Jennie was not going to be talking to her any more that night and she knew it.

Elaine was thinking that Jennie was becoming a handful. What could be the problem? She hoped it wasn't a situation to do with the neighbours across the street. It really began to bother her.

Elaine and Doug were both becoming very concerned but couldn't determine what the problem was. Jennie had changed considerably since they moved. The changes occurred daily and it was getting worse.

Next day...

Verna, the sitter, called Elaine at work. "Elaine, you need to come home now. Jennie is talking about things that are just wrong. The girls are playing in ways that seem sexual. I think things are happening in the house across the street that aren't right. I am sorry, but I just feel it."

Elaine could hardly get home fast enough. They lived in the country and the trip seemed as though it took three hours and not the 30 minutes it usually takes. She ran into the house and the sitter was sitting in the kitchen, waiting for her. Jennie was in the living room watching TV.

Nancy was sent home because of their type of play and chatter. The girls were playing quietly and talking about the stick game again and whom they would be playing the game with the next day. They said that Nancy's grandfather would be visiting and they could play the stick "game" with him too (Predators often refer to their twisted activity as a game or play to the victim as a part of grooming). The babysitter, again, asked the girls what the stick game was and how they played it - the girls wouldn't tell her, just that they each played alone in a room with the adults. When the sitter told Elaine, she agreed with the sitter regarding her interpretation of the stick game. It was causing great anxiety for everyone.

As soon as Doug got home, Elaine said they had to move. Things with Nancy's mother were getting out of hand and Jennie was becoming increasingly remote from the family and rebellious against their parental direction. She explained that Jennie had mentioned at least twice that Nancy's mother was a better parent because she didn't work. Doug was becoming outraged. He was upset about the comments as well but had no idea where to turn. They both believed that if there were activity in Nancy's house that was abusive to Jennie, they would have to be very careful. The members of Nancy's household may be engaging in criminal activity, which would endanger Jennie and the entire family. Elaine and Doug agreed that moving may be necessary at some point, but they would monitor the situation and see what they would do.

He mentioned to Elaine that another girl in the neighbourhood, Jessica, another four-year-old, had been going to Nancy's house to play, sometimes, at the same time as Jennie was going. He asked Elaine what she knew of Jessica and how their parents might be viewing the situation.

Elaine agreed and stated, "We have to call Jessica's parents and ask them if they have similar concerns. I think there is something drastically wrong in Nancy's house."

Doug and Elaine agreed to call Jessica's parents, Jacob and Samantha, to have a meeting the next day. Jacob and Samantha seemed anxious to have a meeting, too, because they had concerns as well.

Jessica's parents arrived at 8:30 p.m. after the children were in bed. They were fortunate to have an older daughter who could look after Jessica while they were meeting. Elaine and Doug had all of the children in bed when the other parents arrived. They met in a family room with the French doors closed to keep their conversation private.

"So, Jacob and Samantha," Doug began, "we are quite concerned about what might be going on at Nancy's house. Jennie has had behaviours that have become a bit upsetting to us. Is this something you might have experienced with Jessica as well? Or are we giving you new information?"

Both Jacob and Samantha looked at each other quietly and did not seem to be surprised. They admitted that their daughter, Jessica, was acting very strangely as well. They were becoming increasingly concerned but had wondered if it was their parenting. They, too, had experienced the phrase "Show me your privates".

Elaine and Doug told them that their concerns began about four months previously. Jennie had become difficult, loyal to Nancy's mother, was having health issues, and using language not consistent with her age level. Jacob and Samantha said they had had the same types of issues in their home with Jessica. She had become very quiet and seemed remote from the rest of the family. Instead of being difficult in behaviour, Jessica was becoming very quiet to an alarming level. She rarely talked to the family. She seemed to be robotic in behaviour, did what she was told without emotion, and seemed to hate school. She had always liked school.

All parents agreed that the police should be involved. They were very nervous about this prospect, but they knew they couldn't approach Nancy's family about it. Having to act secretively made them afraid. Elaine and Doug said they would call the police and see what the next step should be.

All of the parents were in a state of disbelief. No parent wants to think that their child has been abused by anyone, and certainly not by neighbours. Their daughters all played together and would be at Nancy's house for no more than two hours at a time.

All agreed that play time at Nancy's house must be terminated immediately. They knew their daughters would be upset, but there was no other choice. They hoped the police would act quickly before Nancy's family became aware.

In order to not make it too obvious, Nancy was permitted to come to their houses and play, under strict supervision by parents and sitters. All agreed that this was the solution and to make sure that the people in "that" house weren't alerted to any suspicions.

CHAPTER 3

POLICE

Elaine called the police the next day. She was extremely emotional, and a meeting was arranged at the police station for that afternoon. The officers were concerned and asked if they could meet with the parents immediately.

When Elaine arrived, she was asked to sit in the waiting room for the next detective. It seemed as though it took hours, but it was only about fifteen minutes. A female officer came out of the main office area and escorted her to an interview room. When Elaine told her what had been happening, the officer was quite cool and unemotional. She told Elaine she would have to interview Jennie. Elaine was reluctant and said she would call her husband to make sure it was okay.

Both parents agreed that the interview should happen. Jennie may not say anything, but it needed to be done. When Elaine told Jennie, she said she would be talking to a really nice lady.

Elaine called her sister, Beth, to tell her about what was going on with Jennie and the neighbours. It was very difficult to share. Beth was shocked and very protective of Elaine, Jennie, and the whole family. She told Elaine that she would do whatever the family needed. She felt close to Jennie, and would be there to help in any way. There always seemed to be a bond between Beth and Jennie. They were alike in many ways.

Jennie said she wanted Beth to be there when she spoke with the officer. Jennie knew Beth was coming for a visit. The police confirmed that having Beth in the meeting might be of benefit to Jennie.

When Beth arrived, she learned more details of what the two families were going through and was even more upset. All of the little girls were only four years of age. Beth had experienced teaching children who had been sexually abused. She always consulted school student records in such cases, even though not all information was accessible by teaching staff. She found the situation with Jennie and Jessica disgusting and heartbreaking. She knew from her own experience, that the girls would face a hard future.

"Of course, I will go in with Jennie. I am honoured that she wants me there and that you and Doug will allow it." Beth kept her emotions in check out of respect for Elaine and Doug. She really had a bad feeling about it. She had noticed a change in Jennie as well, even in the short time she had been there for her visit.

The day arrived to go into the police station for the interview. Elaine, Beth and Jennie were the only ones to attend. Too many people would have caused more concern for Jennie. Elaine and Beth gave each other their usual "I'm nervous" look and entered the room.

The minute they entered the interview room, Jennie jumped up on Beth's lap, which just warmed her heart. Beth gave her a big hug, and then the detective entered the room. She asked Jennie questions about her friend, Nancy, and what they did when she was visiting. Jennie said nothing that would indicate wrongdoing on the part of Nancy's family. She talked about their play times and never once indicated that there was anything done that would be uncomfortable.

Beth thought there should have been more questions asked. For example, do you have any secrets with Nancy or her mother? Do you ever feel uncomfortable in Nancy's house? Where do you play? Who is there when you are playing? She thought the detective was untrained regarding child interviews.

After the interview, the police explained that the initial interview questions should not lead a child for responses. The officer has to build a "trust" with the child. They said there is a process involved. Beth and Elaine then understood the reasons for the approach of the officer. They appreciated help from the police even more.

The one thing that Jennie said that shocked Elaine was when Jennie mentioned being in a hidden room. The officer did not ask her to explain the room further to make sure she did not to lead the child. Jennie said that there were lots of people in the room and movies. She said that Nancy's mother used to watch movies in the room. Elaine had never heard about the room. Jennie was so non-communicative with the family, that Elaine wasn't surprised.

The interview lasted about 45 minutes. Elaine and Beth thanked the detective for her time. She told them she would be in touch soon.

Both women were exhausted after the interview. It was heartbreaking to see little Jennie having to go through all of this. They talked about the room that was hidden. Elaine told Beth she had never heard of it. Beth was even more concerned but reserved comment. She could see that her sister was extremely upset.

Next day...

Elaine received a call from the police detective. The detective assured Elaine that children rarely speak of such events because predators instill fear very early in the grooming of children. She assured Elaine that action would be taken. Elaine asked her about the hidden room in the house. The detective said she had taken notes and that it would be a consideration in the investigation.

Elaine called Beth with the news. Beth was very pleased and hoped it would happen very soon. She asked Elaine to keep her posted.

The family believed that the investigation would begin immediately. They hoped it would because Nancy's family would become more aware of the situation because Jennie was no longer permitted to go to Nancy's house for playtime. Jennie was becoming even more agitated and difficult because of this.

Elaine and Doug believed they would have to move. After the police interview, Elaine and Doug were very concerned that there might be retaliation from Nancy's family if they were suspicious. Nancy's mother, father, grandfather and some uncles were lived in the house or visited often. Elaine and Doug were warned by the police that if Nancy's family knew about the police investigation, they might have a threatening situation. The move would have to be done for the safety of the entire family and to remove Jennie from the source of the abuse.

Unfortunately, the police took four months to get the search warrant, which isn't unusual. They found computers and movies under a stair-well behind a false wall. So, there was a hidden room. Crimes in which digital devices are used were fairly new in the mid 1990's. The FBI started recording and studying the crime of digital child pornography in 1993, because the digital product of child pornography was just becoming known. When Beth was a network administrator during the 1990's, computers and devices were simpler than today. Child Pornography existed, computers and devices were used to produce and distribute it, but not with the degree of ease in today's digital world. At the turn of the 21st century, animated gifs were just being introduced to the Internet. Pictures were being transferred by email. Secret websites for child pornography predators increased, but the knowledge of them by the general public was fairly limited. This crime is far more prevalent in today's technological environment.

The officers said they would have difficulty investigating all of the evidence because of staffing and time constraints. This was the norm in the early nineties – the digital crime of child pornography was not as prevalent in that time period. This type of response would never be tolerated in the maturing digital world of today because the crime is better known. All videos would be reviewed. Computers and digital devices have increased the ease with which predators can communicate with each other. Technology has made it economical and easier for predators to access the pictures. At any one time on the Internet, it is estimated there are approximately three quarters of a million predators searching for child pornography sites.

The disappointment of the families about the lack of investigation was indescribable. A few years later, they learned from Jennie that both girls had been threatened: their daddies would be shot, their families would be hurt, they would be hurt, and the list went on. Not only was Nancy's mother involved, but the father, grandfather, and others were too. The girls spoke of a hidden room where they "played". The "postman" would always deliver packages to the home and pick up packages. The packages always contained movies. They never did find out who the postman was, but they suspected he was a delivery person for the videos.

There was no other place for the families to turn. They had to pick up the pieces and forge on with their lives. Both families moved from the subdivision. They had to remove themselves from the environment so that the girls might have a chance to develop without the memories, and away from a potentially dangerous environment.

Elaine and Doug moved to another area within the city. Their new home was in an area that was familiar with the family and one they could trust. They were always accepted in the neighbourhood. Jessica's family moved to another city. They kept in touch for a while and Jessica's family came back to let the girls play together sometimes.

Jennie eventually followed the path of so many sexually abused children. She fell in with the wrong crowd with drinking, drugs, and late-night parties. It was a difficult time for her parents. She was even more defiant and becoming a bit violent.

Elaine and Doug had to make a decision to have her put in a group home because of the effect on the family and her three siblings. The night she was admitted to the group home, she left. When the group home called, Elaine and Doug were absolutely distraught. The staff explained that youth that go into the home are not in a jail, and are free to leave if they want to do so. Doug went out to the streets to find her, which was a very dangerous undertaking. Jennie's friends were street people and very difficult to deal with. Jennie had been spending a lot of days, and sometimes nights, on the streets with her new friends. She even slept on park benches to stay with her friends and party.

After she left the group home, Jennie had gone to visit her sister, Judy, not far from where they lived and told her she would be going to a city close to their home for a little while. Judy called Elaine and Doug to tell them what Jennie had said. They were beside themselves. Elaine went to the city and drove around all of the streets where she thought she could find her daughter. It was a futile exercise, but Elaine thought she could not stay home and just wait for word. She had to do something.

When Beth found out about it, she told Elaine to forget about the city she was searching– she believed Jennie would be heading to a different province. Elaine didn't want to believe Beth. Beth put flyers up in the Salvation Army home for street people in the city in Ontario where she lived, and asked them to please call if they found her. The staff gave permission to post the flyer, but said quite often "runaways" stay away from facilities like the Salvation Army for fear of being caught. They know that would be the first place the police and parents would go to find a juvenile.

Within a week, Jennie was located. She and her friends had stolen a car from a friend's mother. She had stolen a plate from her sister's car to put on the stolen car so that it would be hard to detect. She had, in fact, gone to Ontario with her friends on an adventure. In later years, she told Beth that she had been in her home city, too. Beth knew that was the case but just wasn't able find her.

Jennie and her friends had been busking to get money for food, and sleeping in the car. They washed their hair in Wal-Mart washrooms. The family heaved a huge sigh of relief when she was found. They then had to deal with the ramifications of her actions after she had run away from the group home. Luckily, she was a minor and adult charges were not laid.

Jennie had many emotional challenges as a teenager, resulting from her abuse by the neighbours when she was a child and started living a life-style that was not familiar with the family. Nothing made her feel better or helped her get rid of the memories.

She began living with different people. After a while, she started living with a boyfriend. He tried to kill her by beating her. He wouldn't let her out of their apartment. A neighbour called the police. Elaine and Doug were called and flew to the apartment as fast as they could. When they arrived, Jennie was in a fetal position in the back seat of the police car, protecting her badly bruised face and body. The boyfriend had beaten her so badly that her parents didn't recognize her. She had to live with Elaine and Doug for a while because of the danger she was in at the apartment. They eventually removed all of her belongings and Jennie moved into another apartment, alone.

Jennie had quit school at the age of 16. After a while, she decided to complete her education. She had a determination that was becoming a positive energy experience rather than the negative energy she had lived in earlier years. Jennie seemed to become more responsible, which made her parents, grandparents, aunts, uncles, and her siblings very proud. She attended a college where she took administrative studies. She became a veterinary assistant and worked for the SPCA.

At the age of 18, she had a baby. She was very careful with her diet during her pregnancy. She was so excited to be pregnant that she wanted to tell everyone. Jennie gave birth to a healthy baby boy, Ben. Elaine and Doug, for many reasons, had to take Ben in because Jennie was having difficulties with her relationships and the responsibilities of caring for a baby.

Eventually, Jennie had Ben over to her apartment for weekends. He always looked forward to seeing his mother. They would pitch a tent in the living room and camp in the apartment. Jennie and Ben would go swimming at the pool or lake, go walking in the local park and have quality time together. These visits were gradual and if Jennie's boyfriend was over, Ben was only permitted to stay one night. The boyfriend wasn't always good with Ben.

Jennie managed to find an apartment that had two separate bedrooms. It was reasonably priced and in a good location of the city. Her mother helped her move in. It was exciting because Elaine was going to rent an apartment down the street so that Ben and Jennie could see each other more often. Ben would have his own room. This was a first step to Jennie having Ben full time. Both were becoming quite happy about it.

The first week they were there, a new friend who had helped her move in, came to the apartment and asked her if she would like to go out for some beers and party. She was ecstatic and Elaine took Ben home with her so that Jennie could have a night with some friends. As always, Jennie had been lonely, and this seemed to be a night that she could see people and have a good time. Jennie said, "I love you Mum." Elaine responded with "I love you too, sweetheart." Elaine and Ben left and Jennie got ready to go out.

At 5:30 a.m. the next day, July 15, 2012, Elaine was in her kitchen and the police came knocking at her door. They told her Jennie had been in a car accident and did not make it. The driver was drunk. One other passenger in the car did not make it, either.

Elaine fell back into a wall. She was alone with Ben and couldn't believe what she was hearing.

The fear that she and Doug had all of these years had come true – Jennie had been killed. They wondered at times if it would be murder, suicide, or drug overdose but never thought of a drunk-driving incident. Elaine couldn't stop crying.

Elaine called Doug, who was working out of town. She called her son, Steve, to see if he could come to her house to help her out. She called her daughter, Judy, and son, Noah. She called her mother. And then...

Elaine called Beth in at 6:19 a.m. and told her the terrible news. Beth screamed and began crying immediately. The devastation was indescribable. She could only think of poor Jennie and then cried out, "Poor

Ben!" She yelled out to her husband, "Mike, Jennie was killed in a car accident. Oh my God!" She called her son and told him. He was in total shock, too.

Beth and her husband got into their car within two hours and drove to Elaine's to help support the family and attend the funeral. Beth was hysterical, and drove most of the way home crying. She insisted on driving because it kept her mind occupied. Mike kept navigating and they managed to get there within 1.5 days, about 1,200 km.

Jennie was a victim of two major crimes – child pornography and drunk driving. Beth kept thinking about it. What a horrible time for the entire family, particularly Elaine, Doug, their other children, and in particular, Ben. Poor Jennie...

How can so many dark situations happen to one family? The loss was incredible. Beth's and Elaine's sister had been lost to cancer and the same sister's son died in a plane crash just two years before she died. Cancer death, plane crash death, child pornography victims, drunk driving death.

The funeral for Jennie was so quiet and emotional. Everyone was in disbelief. Ben was only four and did not understand the meaning of death. He did not attend the funeral. It took Elaine and Doug at least four years to explain that he would never see his mother again.

Many people attended. Elaine and Doug held it in a downtown church, so that all of Jennie's friends could attend. The family gathered outside the sanctuary. Her younger brother had selected a song for the processional. Everyone quietly followed the casket as it rolled down the aisle. Tears were flowing. Newscasters had covered the accident across Canada. The recessional song for leaving the church did not play because of a technical problem. It was so quiet when everyone left the church. It was deafening.

At the burial, Doug drove their car to the gravesite and the song was broadcast from the car. Doug, Elaine, and Beth held each other as it was played. Beth was sobbing. Doug and Elaine found the music comforting. As they stood listening to the music, a butterfly fluttered around them, flew up, and dropped directly in front of them. Everyone noticed it. Jennie loved butterflies and saw them as a wonderful representation of the beauty and freedom in nature. The butterfly stayed with the three of them until the music ended. Maybe it was Jennie's spirit.

Three months after the funeral, Elaine, Doug, and Ben flew to Saskatchewan. Ben kept looking out the window, for hours. He finally sat back, put his head down, and said, "I can't see Mommy. Everyone said she was in the sky in heaven and I can't see her." This was extremely emotional for the family.

Elaine and Doug adopted Ben so they could keep him in the family and continue to parent him. They have never regretted this. He is the joy and apple of their eyes. His eyes are identical to Jennie's, which is both difficult but comforting to them. Elaine and Doug, their children, Beth, all members of the family will never be the same after such a tragic end to a very troubled life. Jennie had only four years of innocence in her young, 22-year life. What a travesty.

CHAPTER 4

CHARLENE AND HER EXPERIENCES

I, too, have had negative experiences involving sexual assault, but at ages 15 and 21, much older than the age of four when Jennie was sexually abused. I have first-hand knowledge regarding how much these types of traumas can affect someone for the rest of their life. Trust becomes a great issue. I can identify with sexual assault victims because of my experiences. Readers will come to realize that these true stories have a tremendous negative impact on the lives of the victims and their families.

One of the worst incidents in my life occurred when my high school teacher sexually assaulted me. I was on a school trip with a teacher and another student, Betty. We were there with a club from the high school, and were in discussions about international issues involving youth. There were students from across Canada.

Betty and I were billeted in different homes. It was nice because the billet families could speak French – both homes had only French-speaking families. The supervising teachers stayed a hotel in the French City. The hotel sits on the sea and has a beautiful architecture and view.

After three days, Betty and I decided we wanted to put our money together and stay at the hotel, where our teacher supervisor was staying. We thought it would be an adventure and were excited.

We called the hotel and were able to obtain a two-bed room at a reasonable price. We apologized to our billeting families and went to the hotel. I was pleased because my host family drove me to the hotel. I felt as though I had insulted them, but the adventure was just too great to pass up. The hotel was magnificent.

The father shook my hand, and said "Bon chance," which means "good luck". It was a friendly parting and he seemed to realize that the opportunity would be fun for us. I still felt badly about leaving – they were a great family.

We told our teacher, Mr. Stu Pid (Mr. S.), we were going to be staying at the hotel. Mr. S. was about 40 years of age, dark hair and slightly balding. He stood about 6 foot 2 inches tall. He was very pleased we would be staying at his hotel, asked for our room number and said he would stop by later to check on us. We felt safe because our teacher would be in the same hotel. The adventure seemed to be going very well.

When Mr. S. came to the room, I was alone. I was sitting on the bed wearing my favourite blue jeans and a red shirt. Betty had gone shopping with a girl she had met from Vancouver. Mr. S. decided to sit down, held my hand, and talked to me. His hand began to move up my arm and to my chest. His actions made me feel extremely uncomfortable. He asked me if I wanted to be silly. He said, "Let's get silly on the bed and have some fun!" I immediately removed his hand and just looked at him and said, "What do you mean by silly?" He grabbed my hand again and hugged me, "Oh, just silly, you know. You are the nicest and prettiest young girl I know." I responded with "No, I don't know. Please take your hand away...now." I pulled his hand away and pushed him off me. Mr. S responded with, "You know, maybe we should leave the room and go somewhere. I can hardly help myself." I was quite happy to leave the room. I was just sick to my stomach.

I began to clue in that he was suggesting sex. I became extremely nervous. He took my hand and asked to go out on the fire escape. I went with him. He was very dominant and I thought at least we were out of the bedroom. He put his arms around me and gave me a kiss on the lips as he was massaging my chest. I was disgusted and completely repulsed – he was ugly and his breath reeked. I pushed him away and he grabbed me again. I pushed him and told him to stop and left the fire escape. I was crying inconsolably.

He followed me and turned me by my shoulder. I started crying, looked at him and said, "You need help. I am not interested in you so please stop! I have a boyfriend and you are my teacher. What is your problem? You don't get it?"

He started to say something. I walked away and told him not to bother. I wasn't the least bit interested. He asked me to turn around because he had something he needed to say. I wiped my eyes, turned around, and blurted "Like what?"

He begged me to not tell anyone – it would cost him his job, his marriage, and everything else. I said I wouldn't tell anyone but to please leave me alone. The thought of telling anyone would have been very embarrassing for me.

The whole experience caused me stress and anxiety. I wished I had never decided to stay at the hotel. After the trip, I had to take a history course from him until the end of the year. It was a long few months, but I passed the course. I still couldn't get over that a teacher would behave like that. My father, mother, sister, and grandmother were teachers and I had never heard of a teacher being so unprofessional.

I spoke with my mother about the assault. She said to not tell my father because it could escalate to a level that might not be comfortable for me. To this day, I am grateful that I did not go further with it. However, I learned about 25 years later that Mr. S's brother, also a teacher, was charged with assaulting young girls.

Four years later, when in university, I was in a lab, alone, completing a large assignment. It was at 6:30 p.m. in January. There was a snowstorm outside. I thought I should leave soon but needed to complete the assignment. I was walking, so getting home wasn't the issue it would have been had I been driving. The building was at the top of the hill. Going home downhill would be even easier.

My professor, Professor Pred Ator (Prof. P.), came into the lab. I could smell beer on his breath and his hair was messy. He came over and asked me what I was doing. I explained that I was finishing the assignment because it was due the next day.

He came closer to me, which made me feel uncomfortable. I started feeling the same way I did in high school with Mr. Stu Pid. I started to get extremely angry. He pulled up my shirt, touched my breast and tried to kiss me. This time, I pushed him hard, told him to get away and went running out of the lab. I wasn't going to let the creep get away with it. I had such a rage – two times? Really? I had flashbacks of the incident in high school, which raised my anger to rage.

I ran all of the way home crying. I couldn't believe that it happened again. My run down the hill was with energy I didn't know I had. This time, I wasn't going to let another pervert off with it. He claimed to be a good religious man but his behaviour illustrated otherwise.

I told my mother and father about it. I was older and thought I would deal with it differently. They were both shocked and concerned.

I talked about the incident with a Sociology Professor I respected. He reported it to the Board of Governors. I experienced, as do many girls, being treated as a liar and a cause of the incident. It was quite alarming to be treated that way. My integrity has always been unquestioned and to be treated as though I was not telling the truth was quite disturbing. To be treated as though I had solicited his behaviour was enraging. My reaction to his moves should prove that solicitation was not the case, right?

Unfortunately, too many women are treated this way in society. And, unfortunately, too many predators of children treat their victims this way. They sometimes will say the child gave them the indication that they wanted sex. Realize that, as a victim of this type of assault, and having a young child in the family having been assaulted, it is vile and victimizing that anyone would say a victim "wanted" it. Reporting an assault and enduring the criticism and accusations illustrates that a victim would not be asking for the advances. A young, innocent child would never "ask" for advances either.

I was worried the professor might fail me because of the report. I managed to get through my fourth year of university and graduated in the First Division, with honours. This was done in spite of the incident and in spite of the trauma I had experienced emotionally. I later found out that the professor was told that any negative behaviour toward me would be recorded on his personnel file. The Board of Governors gave him that message. They at least helped by disciplining him without publicity, which gave me validation that I was believed.

Not until ten years later did I find satisfaction. The professor who assaulted me had a number of complaints lodged against him and was removed from the staff of the university. At least I had information that other females had complained about him and been believed. I believe I made a difference by being the first to report it.

These kinds of experiences destroy the victim's trust in other people. To have this type of assault occur twice had made me suspicious of people in positions of authority. My experiences in life helped me to understand Jennie so well. Jennie was a textbook case of a child who had been sexually abused at an early age and had negative ramifications through her teens and early adulthood. My experience happened when I was older but began at the age of 15 – still a child. Even though older, I still knew how it could have a negative impact on Jennie.

I have held many positions working as a computer/network specialist. In one part-time, contract position, I would fix and reimage the machines. "Reimaging" involves formatting the hard drive of a computer and installing a new operating system on the machine – no previous user files will exist on a hard drive after formatting and reimaging. I reviewed the machines and repaired and reimaged them daily for distribution.

When reviewing one machine, I was puzzled about the pictures that were on the hard drive. I decided to do a .jpg search of the machine before reformatting. This is fairly easy to do – the command in DOS is dir *.jpg. When the command is entered, all picture files that have a .jpg extension are listed. I also tried dir *.bmp, another type of picture file. A technician was with me when I did the search. We both froze as we sat looking at the pictures. The pictures were of young children (approximately four years of age) in sexually explicit positions. The Canadian Criminal Code is very clear about these types of pictures being defined as child pornography. Viewing them was very disturbing. The computer and evidence were taken from the office and to the proper authorities by the technician. The whole experience was unnerving to both my colleague and me.

The effect of seeing such pictures was difficult. Counselling became a necessity. The flashbacks of the pictures haunted me. Flashbacks are very difficult to deal with – the pictures I had come across kept reappearing in my mind over and over again. I have never remembered specifically how many pictures, just that there were several. There was one picture of a four year old in particular that haunts me to this day. The little girl reminded me of Jennie. I would frequently leave my workstation and cry because of the flashbacks. I did not understand what was going on, just that the continual remembrance of the pictures was haunting. I wondered how police in a child exploitation unit could cope with seeing these pictures.

How could anyone commit such heinous acts? People, who view child pornography, whether or not they have been involved in the actual abuse, are abusers themselves. They are contributing to the abuse by accessing, sharing, and viewing the pictures. Those who view such pictures are contributing to the child pornography industry, an industry that has hurt families terribly.

CHAPTER 5

CHARLENE, A VICTIM

I became very upset after dealing with the pictures. Trying to cope with the flashbacks became very painful. I found my emotions very difficult and left my work post many times with uncontrollable crying. I made an appointment with my physician. "Dr. O" was very sympathetic and told me that I needed to leave the workplace for a while. I took a week-long leave of absence to see if that would help.

My doctor gave a diagnosis of PTSD. I had to ask her what it meant. She explained that it was Post Traumatic Stress Disorder. After the diagnosis, I started realizing the PTSD acronym was being used all the time, connected to many traumatic incidents in society, not just war. I began to understand that the results of seeing the pictures, having so many flashbacks, and being woken in the night from nightmares were all related to PTSD.

I believed that no one could ever understand why I felt so terrible. One can try to overcome abuse, but eventually the feelings of worthlessness, despair, and horror surface and take over. My experiences with the teacher and professor, along with Jennie's horrendous experience, also contributed to my feelings of hopelessness and despair. Who can you trust?

Jennie and I both endured victimization. Jennie was a direct victim and I was a vicarious victim. The diagnosis "PTSD by proxy" was given because I felt the pain and anxiety of the children I viewed in the pictures. The trauma is different for each, but PTSD prevails regardless. Seeing the pictures and having flashbacks daily are difficult. Being a direct victim would be even worse.

I attended many courses related to overcoming the symptoms of PTSD: three mindful-meditation courses and yoga. All of my educational experiences contributed to helping me overcome many of the emotional challenges of living with PTSD. Without this education, I believe I would have been overtaken by the dark and depressing emotions associated with having lived through a trauma.

Because of allergies to all medications related to alleviating the symptoms of PTSD, and having to overcome the feelings through natural health remedies, my doctor and I decided I had to leave the work place indefinitely, which certainly helped. It didn't matter where I was; the memories of the experiences were always present.

I thought about options, and decided to study holistic nutrition to see if there was any other way I could recover. I had been going to an organic store and the manager seemed very knowledgeable. I asked the manager what she had studied and she told me she had studied holistic nutrition at a college in our city. The manager said nutrition could help many issues. Holistic nutrition includes the study of body, mind and spirit. Different foods or food groups can affect skeletal, general health, and emotional issues. Very few people realize this. The severe anxiety experienced was extremely difficult to overcome without help. Prescription medications were not an option.

I enrolled in a Registered Holistic Nutrition program in Toronto, Ontario, an in-depth program with many courses on natural ways of treating disease. Included in the program were courses in anatomy, chemistry, physiology, nutrition, and others. The holistic program included the comparison of religions, and emotional studies.

I completed the two-year course in six months. I was addicted to learning. I realized that the information would be invaluable to me in my difficult situation. My emotions gradually became more positive and my goals more energetic. Food, regular walking with mindfulness, and organic supplements helped me to acquire this energy.

My mother came to Toronto to attend my graduation ceremony, as did my son, his financee (now wife) and my husband. I asked the family if they wanted to leave early to avoid the Toronto traffic rush. As we were leaving, the Head of the school asked us to stay. She said they had something to present to me. A professor asked me to go on the stage to receive the Award of Excellence. This experience did so much for my emotional health. I believed that, finally, someone recognized my strengths. It started a new chapter in my life of "trust". It has been very gradual and a long journey.

After graduation, I enrolled in a graduate course related to nutrition and emotional difficulties. In other words, nutrition related to mental health. It became obvious to me that many people who are bipolar, anxious, depressed, or on medications for these or similar conditions, may need changes in nutrition. When I began my nutrition practice, I had clients with emotional challenges who benefited from better nutrition choices through my counselling.

Based on my changes in diet, and developing a nutrition practice wherein I was helping many people with their health issues, I was able to overcome the dark side of PTSD and enter a very positive growth stage. I turned many negatives into positives by channeling my energy to applications that are of benefit to society. I will always be very grateful that I studied nutrition and was able to improve my emotional health through organic and nutritional means. The allergy to the medication could have ruined any chances for my recovery. My choice to study holistic nutrition and work towards better health made a huge difference for me.

After I began feeling better, I started to review the history of the families and all of the incidents that caused so much anxiety for all family members. It was interesting that once I began to feel better emotionally, I started realizing that all members of the families were suffering. Jennie's life and death caused so much devastation for everyone involved. We have all wondered how one human being should have to endure so much.

One day I woke up and asked myself, "What can I do to help families overcome this horrific experience?"

CHAPTER 6

PLANNING THE CHARITY "CHILD PORNOGRAPHY HURTS"

Elaine has never been the same since Jennie passed. Nor has the entire family. There is a hole in the family that will never be mended.

Everyone loved Jennie so much and wished her life had been different. Jennie had just begun to change and tried to mend the mistakes in her life before the drunk driver killed her.

I studied and researched various ideas or activities that I could engage in to change things or to make things better for the family.

In April 2014, just under two years after Jennie was killed (July 2012), the trial for the drunk driver took place. Elaine and Doug were going to the hearing and viewing very traumatic details about how their daughter was killed. I believed I should be there to give them support through such a horrid experience. About one month before the trial, I called Elaine and told her I would be going home for the trial. Elaine was very pleased and surprised. The judge and jury would see us sitting together with the rest of the family.

When I arrived, my mother drove me directly to the courthouse. The court was in recess. When Elaine saw me, she came over to me slowly, hugged me, and sobbed. I will never forget it. The defence lawyer, and the defendant accused of killing Jennie, looked at each other and laughed. I will never forget that either. Their callous reaction was shocking. It was all I could do to refrain from yelling at them. Elaine didn't see them laughing; she will have to read this book to know it.

I met the parents of the other passenger killed in the accident. The driver survived, as did his girlfriend. It was very difficult to see two families having to live through the trauma again, in a courtroom. Lawyers and forensic specialists described the injuries that the victims had to endure, using verbiage and pictures.

At one point in the trial, the court social worker informed Jennie's family there would be pictures shown of Jennie at the accident scene and post-mortem. Elaine and Doug tearfully said they would stay in the courtroom. I told them if they were staying, then I would stay. I knew it would be a difficult time but was willing to endure it in support of Elaine and Doug.

The pictures were horrendous. At one point, the defence lawyer focused on something red in the grass and asked that the picture be enlarged. He stated that it should be known to the jury that it was the hair of the victim and not blood. He seemed to want to make it prominent so that seeing blood in the grass wouldn't influence the jury. This was most unfortunate. It was very hard on the family. I had to put my head down and wipe the tears. Jennie had her hair dyed red. It was a huge part of her hair that had been ripped off her head after the car had flipped three times, landing in the ditch.

The trial experience made me more determined to do something to help the family, in particular, Elaine and Doug. I returned home after the trial and decided to get to work on an idea that I thought might help all of the family.

I thought of the many difficulties the family had experienced, including my own experiences. Many of the issues were surrounding child sexual assault and the resulting emotional trauma. I started looking into organizations that helped victims of child pornography. The only organizations I could find helped only with child sexual assault.

I believed that the victim of child pornography had to be treated differently than a victim of child sexual abuse. The victim of child sexual abuse experiences the trauma within a confined geography. It is usually in a room, or a location that is not necessarily shared with other people. I knew through conversations with Jennie, that Jennie had been tortured with the idea of wondering what pervert was looking at her picture at any given time. I wondered how I could start an organization devoted solely to victims of child pornography?

A friend of mine told me I should contact child exploitation units within various police forces. This was sound advice. When I called my first choice, I was nervous. This was all new to me. Several Canadian national, provincial, and municipal police forces were consulted.

The first police supervisor I spoke to seemed very receptive to my inquiry. He thought the concept of a supportive organization for victims was a good one. I had completed some research and developed a slide show presentation that could be presented to the public, as a start to an educational component of the organization. I believed that in order to help victims, the organization should have a proactive approach to the crime by giving educational sessions to parents, caregivers, and professionals in an attempt to improve child protection methods. I also believed that parents were failing to realize the necessity of rethinking their parenting skills to include digital activities of their children. The supervisor referred me to an officer who was very helpful. This was a good start. The officer travelled to a police station close to my home to review my presentation, which I found very encouraging. The police in this child exploitation unit have given Child Pornography Hurts excellent support. The unit works with a large number of cases within Canada and has a worldwide reputation of excellence.

The officer's main comment was that my approach was different, but that he liked it. He has remained in contact, and answers my questions about the Canadian Criminal Code, and crimes. This officer and unit have been invaluable to the preparation and continuance of the organization.

I decided to call one particular national police organization, in Ottawa, regarding child exploitation. Without knowing specifically whom I should contact, I made inquiries, and kept getting my call passed on to someone else. I finally spoke with an officer who gave me the number of her supervisor and transferred the call.

The supervisor was very friendly. I told him that I was contemplating starting a charity that would help victims of child pornography, by paying for and arranging their much-needed therapy. The charity would also provide workshops and seminars to the public to see if it could educate children and families regarding the crime and the proliferation of digital child pornography.

He was very interested and stated that if the organization was developed, it would help to provide a missing link because no one in the country was actually organizing treatment, education, and linking the crime to law enforcement. He asked me how I got his number because it was reserved for law enforcement only. I realized that perhaps the officer who gave me the number might be in trouble, so I told him I wasn't sure of the name. He stated he was having national conference call and it was to begin within ten minutes. I quickly thanked him for his time. He told me to keep in touch.

His response was very encouraging. Later, the news media included the report of multiple child pornography arrests, Canada wide. The conference call he referred to was related to talking to the media that day.

I met with municipal police forces and child exploitation units to have them review all of the material for presentations. They asked for a copy and I sent them a .pdf file for their review. They went through it in detail and commended me for the research I had conducted.

All the police forces, with which I have been in contact, have been supportive and open to answering any questions I have had regarding crimes, and specific parts of the Canadian Criminal Code.

I went further and had many phone meetings with therapists in New York City, Connecticut, New Hampshire, California, Winnipeg, Toronto, and London, Ontario. The conversations were always productive. Most agreed that there needed to be an organization that would help with both understanding the crime of child pornography and helping victims.

It has been said that the victims of child pornography are "just" victims of child sexual abuse. I would argue this with anyone. These victims are far more than "just" child sexual abuse victims – their pictures are in cyberspace and will be there in perpetuity. Therapy for this type of victimization must be changed to reflect this understanding and the daily trauma these victims endure.

Some researchers have stated that there is little research done to determine the cause of child pornography offenders and the size of threat they pose to children. The treatment for victims is fairly new as well. Many organizations are just beginning to realize that victims of child pornography have recurring trauma, because the pictures or videos are continually being distributed and viewed. The type of therapy required for these victims needs to be specialized.

After research and several discussions with multiple police forces, I began to realize what types of goals I would have for the charity. I decided to meet with a charity lawyer to discuss registering the charity in Canada. The lawyer told me that it would cost about $12,000 to $20,000, and take two to five years to become registered. It was explained to me what charitable objectives are when registering a charity and that the charity I was contemplating should be registered using a charitable objective related to education, based on the objective of educating the public about the crime and issues surrounding digital activities. After leaving the lawyer's office, I began thinking about objectives for the charity and where to go from there.

Three objectives came to mind: 1. Providing and arranging for much needed therapy for child pornography victims; 2. Providing seminars, educational sessions, and the like, to the public, youth, children, and professionals so that the crime of child pornography could be understood, with a goal to fight the crime proactively; and 3. to provide any other services as deemed necessary to accomplish the first two objectives.

The day after the conviction of the drunk driver, who killed Jennie, I sent application papers to Corporations Canada, to have Child Pornography Hurts registered as a not-for-profit corporation. I had approached four people whom I respected and trusted to be the voting members for the Board of Directors. Child Pornography Hurts Inc. was realized as a not-for-profit corporation in Canada, May 14, 2014. I decided that the application to become a registered Canadian charity should be completed as soon as possible, so that the organization could issue charitable donation receipts. It is very difficult to obtain funding and donations without being able to issue an income tax receipt.

I remember receiving the official corporate seal, letters of incorporation, and other papers. It was surreal to me. I was scared but triumphant. It made me think – what will happen if this charity doesn't get off the ground? Will I feel like a failure? Will I feel as though I let the family down?

Not long after the start-up of Child Pornography Hurts, the Board of Directors developed a Twitter account, to be used as an information medium to the public. In November 2014, the board member who managed it called me and stated that he had received a child pornography picture. I was horrified. He asked what he should do.

Through meetings, I knew the Head of a municipal police force child exploitation unit and emailed her immediately. The detective sent an officer to the board member to obtain a statement and information regarding the tweet. The police determined that the tweet originated in a city in the United States. Within one week, I received a copy of an email from Homeland Security of the United States informing me that the nineteen-year-old predator had been arrested and the infant victim had been rescued. Yes, predators have assaulted infants. It was excellent that there was an arrest, but the rescue of a victim was even better.

Anyone with compassion and love for children would be very disturbed by this kind of evidence. I have enormous respect for the police and anyone who works to protect children.

CHAPTER 7

"INTERNET SENSE FOR INTERNET SAFETY"

I have shared with many people that I will always feel indebted to my first board members for their support and time. We began with five voting members (including myself). The Board members believed enough in the charity and me, to commit to being on the board.

The first board meeting with the corporate seal was exciting. All members viewed the corporate seal as evidence that we were really in business. We formally sealed the letters of incorporation then sat down to discuss our progress to date.

The vision of Child Pornography Hurts was finalized:

"Helping victims become survivors; fighting to end child pornography."

The mission statements were finalized:

"To work collaboratively with like organizations, social service agencies and law enforcement so that victims can be identified and given support.

To work collaboratively with all agencies and police to end child pornography.

To provide educational seminars to groups, schools and associations in order to fulfill our vision and mission."

All members of the Board were very pleased with our vision and mission statements. We had thought we would provide gifts and/or a trip for victims as a fourth mission, but the insurance would have been cost-prohibitive, and staffing would have been impossible

A corporation in Southwestern Ontario provided Child Pornography Hurts with our first grant, which helped us to begin our work. I covered all costs, personally, for incorporation, which was about $1,000. I maintain that the cost was immaterial. The cause is the main objective.

After speaking to the charity lawyer, who had informed me that it would cost about $12K to $20K and two to five years to achieve charitable status, I decided that I would research the possibility of becoming a charity on my own. The board of directors was very supportive of this, so I set out and started studying.

I decided that the organization would apply as an educational charity, along with providing therapy support for victims. I wrote the charity's objectives and completed the entire form, which was an arduous, time-consuming task. I asked charity specialist, Hope Clark, if she would be able to review the document. She said she would and the board agreed. She has been, and continues to be, an invaluable support to the organization. I will always be very grateful to her.

Child Pornography Hurts Inc. became a registered Canadian charity, January 14, 2015. The consultant with Canada Revenue Agency was very supportive of the cause and helped with the charitable objectives. It was a day that was very gratifying to all members. When I received the good news that we were approved as a registered charity, I called each board member individually to tell them. It was a triumphant day. Child Pornography Hurts became a registered charity within six months of submitting our initial application!

Soon after, I decided we needed to copyright the term "Internet Sense". The term can be defined as the awareness people need to have for safety on the Internet. The Board of Directors agreed, and we had the copyright completed. I then proposed having a trademark "Internet Sense For Internet Safety", and all agreed.

Initially, the Canadian Intellectual Properties Office refused the proposed trademark. I contacted the office directly. The consultant assigned to our application said he believed in the charity so much that he helped with the verbiage required to have the trademark approved. The charity now has the trademark approved and it is used in all educational presentations.

One time, I was sitting in a meeting and wondering who might endorse the charity. I kept thinking, as the meeting progressed, about Federal Minister Hon. Ed Holder. I thought he might be interested. After the meeting I went to the downtown market and purchased a protein bar for my lunch. After this purchase, I went through a downtown parking lot toward my car.

As I was approaching my car, I noticed a car pull into the space beside me. I walked up to the driver's side, the door opened and, lo and behold, I was looking into the eyes of a person I believed to be Honourable Ed Holder.

We stopped and chatted for a few minutes. I described the charity to him and told him I really needed some guidance and wondered if there might be some sort of support from the government or another organization. He took my business card and told me to call his office the following Monday.

When I called his office the next day, his assistant told me that Hon. Ed Holder was busy and that I might be able to meet with him in a few weeks. When I began to explain the coincidence of the previous day, Hon. Holder's assistant responded with, "Oh yes, Ed gave me your business card. Charlene?" I explained with happiness that, "yes, this is Charlene!"

I met with Hon. Holder that Thursday. He asked that I prepare letters for federal ministers and he would deliver the letters to them personally in the legislature the next week. The letters were to go to three different federal ministers. I dutifully prepared the letters and had them in his hands the following Monday. The Minister of Public Safety sent an extensive letter in which he stated that the safety of all Canadian children is of great concern to the federal government.

Within four months, I had contacted, met with, or corresponded with several members of provincial and federal parliaments. I received letters from several members. Little did I realize that these letters would be profoundly important when applying for funding, both publicly and privately. The learning curve for beginning a charity was sharp, but I believed I was becoming successful. I will always be very grateful to former Honourable Minister of Science and Technology for Canada, Hon. Mr. Ed Holder, for his unbelievable support of Child Pornography Hurts.

Since that time, Hon. Mr. Holder lost his seat in the federal election in Canada in 2015. I have met with his replacement and others within the new government. They have been equally supportive, but the initial act of support from Hon. Ed Holder was the catalyst that helped the beginning of the Child Pornography Hurts and gave me much needed confidence.

To anyone who might have a reason to want to make a change in society, I advise that you follow your soul and your heart. If you want to help others, follow your goals. I have never wanted to be a person with regrets – we have enough regrets in life. When it comes to far-reaching goals, reach for the sky. You never know what you might be able to accomplish.

When my son was 15, he said he thought he would never be a good enough football player to make a university team. I told him "Follow your dreams, reach for the sky. You will never know your potential until you do." He later did follow my advice, and was recruited by several universities to play football. I am, and always will be, thankful my son followed my advice. I see this as one of the greatest gifts my son could have given me.

With the development of the charity, I have had a sense of purpose, which has been very healing for me. Every time there has been a success, Elaine is the first person I call. Elaine is always enthusiastic and supportive. She is in wonderment about the successes that I, and the charity, have had in the amount of time since its inception. It illustrates the absolute need for this organization to help end the horrid crime of child pornography. Parents, caregivers, and professionals need the education the charity can and will provide.

CHAPTER 8

"CHILD PORNOGRAPHY HURTS"

Child Pornography Hurts is a federal Canadian charity, meaning it is a Canada-wide charity, not just designated to a community or province. This designation was necessary because the crime is Canada-wide.

As noted previously, Internet Sense For Internet Safety® is the trademark used for educational sessions. There are four different presentations, which are updated regularly, through media coverage, police consultations, therapist consultations, etc. Child Pornography Hurts strives to be as up-to-date as possible.

The first presentation is for parents, caregivers, and professionals. The way we present is very different from other organizations. There are websites that attempt to educate people on the difficulties of monitoring digital choices of children/youth on the Internet and cellular devices. Through many interviews with adult groups and therapists, it is clear that few people go to these websites to obtain information. The approach of Child Pornography Hurts is different in that we go out to the community and speak personally about the challenges of digital supervision. Adults are then able to ask questions and feel more comfortable about increasing their parenting and supervisory skills to include digital supervision. For some, their computer knowledge and skills are limited. To have a live presentation with someone who has information on the topic means they are better equipped with knowledge and skills to engage in the application of digital supervision.

The second presentation of Child Pornography Hurts is for children and youth. These sessions are designed to educate children and youth about the law and why they should improve their choices regarding Internet and electronic cellular devices. We explain the consequences of their actions, Criminal Code legislation regarding child pornography. We present cases in which children and youth have been charged and convicted for engaging in activities related to child pornography. Also included are the many avenues that predators use to find and groom victims.

The third presentation is to families. In these groups, parents and care-givers would attend with their children and youth. This session would be primarily for the children and youth so that parents can better understand the type of education and needs their children have related to digital activities.

The final presentation is for children aged 8 to 12. Everything is explained in simple terms so that the children will better understand their choices and the safety required when using digital devices and exploring the Internet. Through meetings, the police shared that they have had to deal with children aged 8 to 10 who are producing and dis-tributing child pornography. At this age, they are engaging in selfies of genitalia and breasts and have very little realization of the magnitude of their actions. The parents who own the equipment being used need to realize that there are implications for them as well. It is important to monitor activity because police could be knocking on the door of a parent and asking how pictures ended up on their digital devices.

PART TWO

DIGITAL SUPERVISION AND THEORY

Parenting has become very complex. Parents are very remote from the activities of their children when their children are on various devices. Children spend more time using technology, than they spend with their families and school. The average child spends approximately seven and three quarter hours on digital devices every day. (Parents.com).

We cannot afford to allow our children to be raised without guidance. They are learning more about communication, relationships, and the concept of friendship, through digital devices than with their familial or peer communications.

On the "Every Chance To Learn" website, parents have stated that they have no reference regarding technology and being able to be effective as parents. Some have reported being very perplexed as to where to start when it comes to supervising children when they are on computer related equipment. Before the digital device "epidemic", parents were worried that their children were viewing television excessively and not getting enough exercise. Now, through several discussions with parents, it seems that the television is often used as a discipline tool to remove children and youth from digital devices because of the alarming percentage of their day being consumed by digital devices. Continuous digital activity makes children more susceptible to being targeted by predators.

Digital Supervision is extremely important for parents to understand and implement. It is a theory that will give parents, caregivers, and professionals a road map for the new direction they need to take in child protection and supervision.

The remainder of this book contains information crucial to effective parenting and child protection as related to digital supervision. Criminals have grasped opportunity related to social media and predator activity within so many different environments. This type of criminal is very knowledgeable about the Internet, social media, and digital devices. Children and youth have been engaging in self-exploitive, self-endangering activities. Adults need to learn digital supervisory skills to assist them to be effective as parents, caregivers, and professionals as much as possible in today's digital world.

Too often, adults are allowing a computer, iPad, cell phone or other device to "babysit" their children. Predators and other criminals know this and take great advantage of it. As you read the remainder of this book, you will learn about the crimes associated with the Internet and devices, the activities of children and youth on these devices, and other issues.

Social media are great environments for communications for families, children and their peers, businesses and the like. They have become improved and are new communication tools, especially for families who are separated by distance. However, the reconceptualization of how modern digital media affect children, their safety, and communication behaviours must be realized.

Readers, therefore, you can now understand the definition of "Digital Supervision" as you continue reading on your journey to becoming even more effective as parents, caregivers and professionals with respect to child protection on digital devices.

CHAPTER 9

PARENT AND CAREGIVER CONCERNS

All parents and families are worried about abductions, playground bullying, human trafficking, sex slavery, torture, murder and anything else where children and youth are concerned. Without digital supervision, children and youth can be exposed to all of the above through their independent actions while surfing the Internet, chatting online, playing video games online, etc.

Parents, caregivers, and professionals – would you give your car keys to a 12-year-old and let him or her drive around your city alone, unsupervised? Then, why do you give the key to your router to your children and allow them to drive around the world without your supervision? All parents and caregivers have to realize the extent and risk of travel over the Internet.

Parents have presented many scenarios and questions about the problems that exist with their children and families using computers and digital devices at home and elsewhere, with obvious concerns. Listed below are some common scenarios. In subsequent chapters, digital supervision skills to circumvent these problem areas will be explained:

- Often, parents give their children a code word or phrase so the child to use to determine if a person who approaches them is a safe person. For example, a parent may say the code word is "sports". If the person picking the child up knows the code word, then the child will let the adult accompany them home or drive them in their car.

- Many children have been instructed to use the proper names for their body parts. For example, penis, breast, vagina and others. Many parents have been instructed by professionals to do this so that children will understand the scientific names and be able to describe accurately any activity involving these body parts. This is advisable; however, parents should go a few steps further.

- Parents purchase cell phones for their children. They do this in an attempt to keep their children safe. By having a phone, a child can call their parents or caregivers to make sure the adults who care for them know their location. The cell phone call also be used to access data, if the parent or caregiver decides to purchase a data plan. Data is not always a good idea for children.

- Many homes have a computer in the open area of their home. Parents need to have computer literacy to monitor the activities on the computer and digital devices. Parents do not always monitor the activity in spite of where the computer is located.

- Too often, parents have a basic insecurity related to their knowledge in comparison to the knowledge of their children. They believe they cannot monitor the child and youth.

- Children and youth loan their phones freely to friends or unknown persons, which can cause an unsafe situation.

- Many parents share that their child has told them that "other" kids take nudes of themselves and distribute them electronically to friends.

- Some children, as young as five years of age, are known to have been on pornography sites. Parents find this disturbing and do not understand how the children got to the sites. They require more knowledge to understand this issue and how to avoid it.

- Some spouses have found child pornography on their home computer. They realize that their spouses are guilty of downloading the pictures or videos on the machine. This is problematic in that the children use the same machine. Many wives have stated they do not know what to do and wondered if it was true that the material got on the machine by mistake (as was explained by their spouse). An understanding of the child pornography industry is necessary in order for adults to deal with this type of situation.

- Therapists have stated that youth and some children are addicted to viewing pornography online. This type of addiction can lead to curiosities about child pornography and contribution to the child pornography industry through self-exploitation and sharing of pictures that are of a self-exploitive nature with peers and possibly unknowns. Through digital supervision, this type of activity can be avoided.

- Police have stated that children as young as eight years of age are producing, distributing, and possessing child pornography.

- Police have stated that whenever Child Pornography Hurts makes a presentation that it should be expected there would be child pornographers in the audience – the proliferation of the crime is so prevalent that this is inevitable.

- Therapists have stated they have educated parents on how to disable the cameras on their children's phones. Adults believe that the camera on the phone is the only problem.

- Therapists have stated that some of their clients have claimed to have accidentally accessed child pornography.

- Youth have stated that most students or friends have nudes on their cell phones. It is common, and they believe that they are doing nothing wrong by having nudes of children under the age of 18.

- Youth under the age of 18 have stated they take pictures of their genitalia and breasts regularly, and have distributed them to their electronic followers and friends on social media.

- Children (aged 7 to 12) have taken pictures of their genitalia and breasts using their parents' computers and mobile devices.

- Youth and children have stated that they communicate with absolute unknowns through social media.

- Youth and children have stated that they prefer the social media sites that offer texting and other communications, which claim to provide anonymity. They believe their parents and caregivers will never know about their chats nor confront them about them, nor realize that any images or content can by viewed, saved, or recorded by others.

- Parents are afraid to invade the privacy of the activities of their children. Privacy? Privacy has no boundaries when it comes to child protection.

- Parents and caregivers need to realize how their contributions in social media can affect their entire family. Many parents post on social media regularly about themselves and their families, particularly information about their children. More information regarding the dangers of this activity will be in the ensuing chapters.

- Many children and youth brag about the number of friends they have in social media, the number of followers, etc. They have little awareness of the difference between "real life friends" and "social media friends". Social media has changed the definition of "friend" as it has been understood prior to the introduction of digital devices and social media.

- Child abductors frequent playgrounds, parks, pools, youth organizations, scouts, girl guides, karate schools, neighbourhood gatherings, sports teams, sports events, arenas, religious buildings/organizations, malls, stores, and grocery stores – get the picture? They are everywhere, and now, good at targeting their victims within a ubiquitous playground known as the "Internet".

- Children and adults email recipients unknown to them and have little knowledge of the information they are transmitting via email. Sending emails to unknowns is a dangerous practice.

- Parents and caregivers have stated that it is difficult to instill in children an ability to refuse – to say "no." Parent by example. Teach children that saying no to adults or friends can be okay in certain circumstances.

Most parents, caregivers, and professionals can identify with the statements in this chapter. Most of them are common worries for all parents. As readers continue, digital supervision methods for child protection related to all of the above situations will be explained.

CHAPTER 10

DIGITAL SUPERVISION

Parents, caregivers, and professionals need to "reconceptualize" their definition of child protection and supervision of children and youth. It is advised that the old supervision methods of child protection be supplemented with, and include, "digital supervision."

Previously, various scenarios were outlined related to child protection and parenting methods. You no doubt can identify with multiple scenarios within the chapter. Here, the situations will be explained further, giving parents, caregivers, and professionals ideas required to become current and involved with reconceptualization of child protection and supervision.

Often, parents tell their children a code word or phrase for the child to use to determine if a person who approaches them is a safe person. For example, a parent may say the code word is "sports". If the person picking the child up knows the code word, then the child will go with the adult to a different location, or drive them in their car.

Too often, many parents rely on this "code-word system" safety net and believe they have done everything they need to do to keep their children safe. That has always worked in the past, right? This is the assumption by many parents, an overreliance on this one method of protection.

There are many cases where adults, whom children know, and/or whom they have been instructed to trust, have abducted children. There have also been cases where unknown adults have abducted children. We can never forget the naiveté of children and how much they believe that adults are caring, trusting people, much the same as their parents are (if they have been lucky enough to have such parents as described).

Unfortunately, code words are not enough. In this digital age, too often, parents, as well as their children, have shared personal information about themselves, children, and family activities on social media. Children are not the only ones at fault in this activity. Digital supervision includes the activities of parents and caregivers as well. Parents post pictures regularly about their children, what they have for meals, activities their children are engaged in, accomplishments or failures of their children, and other information. A predator, therefore, has information so personal that abduction becomes too "easy" for them.

A code word or action system would be immaterial when an abductor can approach a child on the street, playground, gym, and recognize them easily from a picture a parent has shared on social media. There is a tremendous risk in not knowing whose eyes are viewing your personal information on social media.

It is an illusion that everything is safe and private on social media. Often users exercise dependence on the established terms and conditions set forth by social media and believe that being able to hide, and not friend unknowns or undesirables, is safe. Users have to realize that information on line is out there, regardless of the social media of choice, and for the use of anyone at any time.

"Sharing" can be very risky online. A person can be described as being "delusional" if they believe everything they do within their social media environment is kept to just their "space". Do parents or relatives always know every "friend" on social media? Unlikely. It is very problematic when anyone befriends an "unknown" online in social media. An unknown can have many reasons for wanting to be a "friend". When you share personal information, an unknown can use the information to their advantage. Please realize, that your "known" friends can be a predator of children as well as your "unknown" social media friends.

Imagine this street scenario: "Your Mom told me you had a bad dream last night. I specialize in bad dreams. She asked that I talk to you about it to see if I can make you feel better. Let's go to my car for privacy, okay? I know your dream involved little Johnny over there because he has been bullying you." The mother had described the sleep issues of her child online. The picture of her child was on a popular social media site. The child would then believe that the parent had a close association with the predator and oblige the request to go to the car. A "code word" would be inconsequential in this type of situation.

Parents also need to realize that sharing personal information about their children in social media can result in bullying of their child by other children. Often, parents have friends in social media who are the parents of the friends of their child. Sharing personal information can be detrimental to the relationships of your child in school. For example, a parent may share the information that their child dislikes being on a school team because the child doesn't like running. Other children could learn about this through their parents, and tease the child. Children could target the child by saying he/she is weak, overweight, lazy, a poser or a "nerd". This is just one example of how much a simple statement in social media could cause bullying issues between children.

Imagine that you share something personal on social media (and many parents do) that your child is being bullied and you don't know what to do. It is devastating to hear your child cry every night. If this information is shared, your child may be targeted even more. Who started the bullying is a question that needs to be asked. The parent sharing the personal information about their child? The parent of another child who shared the information about the bullied child with their child who might be the bully? It is a convoluted situation that must be avoided.

A good word to describe this ongoing sharing and resharing of infor-mation is perpetuation. The innocence of wanting to help by sharing another's info, or making comment on it, may have detrimental effects. It's the "friends of friends" as much as direct friend relationships that people often forget about or are ignorant of. They don't understand how, nor the implication of, the transverseness of how dissemination of information works beyond their singular post.

Many parents lack the realization their child can do harm or bully other children. They also lack the realization some of the parents of their children's friends cannot be trusted. They may share the personal infor-mation about a child which you have shared. Someone else sharing it is beyond your control. It becomes a vulnerable, digital threat to your child and family.

Adults need to be aware of the type of information they are sharing on social media or the Internet. Security on social media is immaterial – there are videos on various sites that teach people how to hack social media, applications, and other sites.

Digital predators now are far more computer literate than the general public realizes. This will be discussed further later.

CHAPTER 11

BODY PARTS AND GROOMING

Many children have been instructed to use the proper names for their body parts. For example, penis, breast, vagina and others. Many parents have been instructed by professionals to do this so that children will understand the scientific names and be able to describe accurately any activity involving these body parts. This is advisable; however, parents should go a few steps further.

Parents are very proud to say they have their children speak about their body parts in real terms. This is very commendable and parents, caregivers and professionals who have decided to teach children this terminology should be applauded.

This is a method developed by professionals and is certainly respected. Real names help when interviewing a child about possible assault or health issues of a child. Parents can ask if a child has been touched using real terms. The child can describe an assault to parents and professionals without confusion as to what might have happened to the child.

Predators are aware of this common instruction to children. They usually avoid discussing body parts by their "real" names. Parents need to be aware of this and instruct their children accordingly. For example, tell their children that some people may use the "wrong" terms for their body parts and to tell their parents if this ever happens.

Parents, caregivers and professionals might, and should, teach children about personal body safety. This is a multicultural challenge. Different cultures will approach the education of personal body safety in different ways. I am suggesting methods of a global nature. Various cultures will need to adapt to these methods within their own parameters. One way to begin to describe personal body safety is to explain to children that body parts covered by a bathing suit or clothing are considered "personal".

Telling children not to allow touching on their personal body parts by another person is extremely important. However, it is equally important to tell children not to touch another person in those body parts as well. In all of the pictures I have seen, no child was being touched by the hands of another person. The child was doing the touching or in a position where body parts of the predator were used rather than hands. This becomes problematic when parents say not to allow anyone to touch them. The child assumes that it is with hands. Parents need to provide clarification that touching should not include hands or other body parts.

It is unfortunate that parents need to explain this type of situation to their children. Discussions with parents have illustrated to me that few parents had told their children to NOT do the touching and to NOT allow touching by body parts, including hands.

Some victims who have been assaulted by child pornographers and child molesters have shared their stories with me. They stated at no time did a predator refer to a penis as a penis, a vagina as a vagina, breast as a breast, and so on. Usually, the body parts were not mentioned, or they were mentioned with a slang term: "peeper" for penis; "opening" as a vagina; "tit" as a breast; etc. The predator treats the situation as a "game" and uses the slang terms to maintain their grooming methods. They may not use terminology at all to keep the "game", within a game type of atmosphere.

As described previously, a teacher sexually assaulted me. I was 15 at the time. I had admired and respected the teacher. Never did he mention body parts nor was he specific about his intentions. He kept saying he wanted to be "silly" and "party". I was naïve and didn't clue in to where the whole conversation was headed until he had taken me onto the fire escape. Looking back, I am sure I was not his first victim and probably not his last. His whole method seemed to be skilled and practiced.

Predators, based on my unfortunate experience and the victims interviewed, are smooth and good at what they do. They are not obvious until they have you in their grasp. This is "grooming." They rarely talk about their intentions or actions prior to engagement. They work on grooming, getting a minor in their trust, and then they become active in some sexual way.

Understanding grooming methods of predators is key for parents to learn how to guide their children. Through research and discussions with victims and police, a list has been compiled of the following possible methods used by predators, either through chats, emails, social media, or in person. They include:

Nudes – predators will often share nude sexual pictures of adults or children to ensure that the victim believes that everything is acceptable. Before the digital age, nude sexual pictures were shared with victims through the use of instamatic pictures or other pictures developed by the predator. After interviewing two male victims, both were shown pictures of predators sexually assaulting victims. The predator would then groom them into believing that the activity was normal and acceptable. Both males still feel totally violated and are coping with the emotional challenges to this day. Both men said the pictures were in the hundreds and in a storage trunk. After asking further questions, both were assaulted in different towns and by different predators.

Finding Things In Common – Predators will tell victims that they "totally understand" what they are going through, particularly with children. A victim might state their friends are all against them or their parents have grounded them for a week. A predator will say they are going through the same thing and try to win them over by having this situation in common with them. This is particularly vulnerable for lonely children or youth who are looking for a "friend". Predators will also identify with the victim with likes and dislikes. For example, if the victim likes skateboarding, so will the predator.

Make The Victim Think What They Want Is Okay – By showing pictures and identifying with the victim, they then work on having the victim believe it is okay to engage in the requested activity because other children and youth have also engaged in it. Younger children are usually shown pictures of nude adults in sexual positions in the beginning of their relationship or communication. The children will become inquisitive about the pictures. Some children are redirected from their gaming site to porn sites to lure them into this type of inquisitive situation. Predators do this digitally. In this type of situation, children are not aware of how they arrived at the porn site. It is rare that a child will tell their parents about viewing these pictures because they believe they might get into trouble.

Agreement – The predator will agree with everything children say. Their victims will believe that the predator knows them best. This will encourage a child to instill trust with the predator. Victims will then begin to agree with requests made by the predator because they believe they have found a "kindred spirit".

Threats – Predators may begin to utter threats. If a potential victim does not go along with their requests, they will say they can share information about the victim to their friends in social media or to their parents. Unfortunately, too often, by the time the threat is given, the victim would have shared pictures or information. The threat is very real at that point and the victim very intimidated.

Flattery, Pity – The predator will never give up. He or she will flatter the victim or give pity related to a child's situation. If the victim sends pictures or videos, the predator can then give them compliments or pity them for their "looks". They may then compare the victim to other people in a positive or negative way, so the victim will then comply with their demands. They target the insecurities of the victim. They can also pity a victim for their situation in life and then use that pity for compliance from the victim.

Parents and caregivers need to share the above-noted forms of persuasion. It is advised that a discussion involving these types of persuasion techniques occur because these grooming methods can also happen between peers, even between boyfriends and girlfriends. This should be considered a part of digital supervision.

CHAPTER 12

ELECTRONIC DEVICES

Parents purchase cell phones for their children. They do this in an attempt to keep their children safe. By having a phone, a child can call their parents or caregivers to make sure the adults who care for them know their location. The cell phone call also be used to access data, if the parent or caregiver decides to purchase a data plan.

Cell phones, webcams, video camera, cameras, and iPads are just some possible sources of self-exploitation of children/youth. These devices are given to children by adults under the presumption they enhance their children's safety, digital knowledge, and technical experience. There is always the risk that an unsafe situation can be the result of using these devices.

Self-exploitation – Children as young as eight are taking pictures of personal body parts and sharing them with friends through electronic cellular devices. This has become a game with children. They think it is funny and love doing it. They are unaware of the risks.

Parents have asked if a meeting can be organized between their children and me to educate their children regarding the negative consequences of some of their digital choices. This is a good idea; however, parents have to be educated as well. Having a meeting with children to educate is excellent. However, parents, caregivers and professionals should experience digital supervision training before their intervention with children and youth on this topic. Without this education, children and youth will still make their own digital choices with the knowledge that their parents have no form of digital supervision. With digital supervision methods, parents can enforce various rules and guide their children on a daily basis.

The Canadian Criminal Code states that anyone in Canada under the age of 18 is considered to be a child. (See reference to the Canadian Criminal Code at the end of this book). When children under the age of 18 decide to use any electronic device to take pictures of themselves nude or of other children under the age of 18, they run the risk of being accused of producing child pornography, even if the pictures are of themselves. When they share these pictures, law enforcement may determine they are guilty of distributing child pornography. In meetings with police, they have shared they have had to deal with children as young as eight years of age who have produced and distributed child pornography. Superintendents of education, principals, and others in education have also made reference to this type of behaviour. Various situations have occurred and involved law enforcement.

Possession of these types of pictures on an electronic device, owned by parents, caregivers, or by professionals becomes more complicated. Adults in these situations may be interviewed by law enforcement. Questions will be asked regarding how the pictures got there, what safety guidelines have been practiced by the adults to ensure the children have been protected. In such interviews, the adults who own the devices are interviewed as a possible predator. Parents, caregivers and professionals are not immune to being predators themselves.

This is a true case. A secondary school principal in Southwestern Ontario interviewed a young female student. She was hysterical that someone had texted (sexted) a picture of her that had been taken at a recent party. She was partially nude and in an intimate position with her boyfriend. The picture had been sent all over the school. She was terrified her parents would find out about the picture and that sharing was continuing beyond the school.

The principal told her she shouldn't have the picture on her phone. He took a copy of her picture with his own cell phone and they deleted the picture on the student's phone. She was grateful the principal now had a copy and might be able to do something about it. The principal called the police. They interviewed her and then the principal.

This is where the legal lines can become misunderstood by citizens. When the principal showed the police the picture on his personal cell phone, they told him he was now in possession of child pornography related to a student within his purview. They explained the Criminal Code and stated he should never have taken a picture of her image on her cell phone with his cell phone. No charges were laid, but it is a lesson well learned: any possession is a criminal offence. The principal was lucky he was not charged.

Digital supervision in this case includes the knowledge of the parents as to data on all devices within their ownership. The adult who owns and pays for devices is responsible for content.

CHAPTER 13

COMPUTER MONITORING AT HOME

Many homes have a computer in the open area of their home. Parents need to have literacy to monitor the activities on the computer and all digital devices. Parents do not always monitor the activity in spite of where the computer is located. Too often, parents have a basic insecurity related to their knowledge in comparison to the knowledge of their children. They believe they cannot monitor the child or youth and feel inadequate.

This section is two-fold: computers should be in an open place in the home. Some parents say they know very little about computers and their children know far more than they do. Supervision in this type of situation is difficult because the parents may have limited knowledge of computers and, therefore, limited ability to digitally supervise their children. Knowledge is power. Many parents have shared their desperation in feeling inadequate regarding the supervision of their children's activities.

Often, parents either know little about computers or they are naïve regarding the activities their children do on the devices. My computer experience includes teaching computer applications, managing a

250-station network and fileserver, managing an email server, repairing computers, developing a windows peer-to-peer network and other computer-related activities. I can realistically share activities that children and youth practice in a school setting. The knowledge students acquire in school from peers, combined with their own experiences related to protecting their own activity on electronic devices, contributes to their self-protection in a home environment.

Many parents know how the computer or iPad is being used – but do they know how to monitor activity?

Be alert that windows or screens can be hidden or minimized, which is how activity can be "hidden" by a device user. This can be very challenging. Parents can observe their children fairly easily with just one computer at home if they follow some child protection guidelines.

When walking by your child sitting at a computer, watch the minimized area of the screen (PC lower left corner; Mac lower right corner). Windows can be minimized so that a person walking by would be oblivious to the actual environment being used by the user. If a window is minimized, pull it back up on the screen by clicking on the minimized icon. When minimized, the website name of the site is abbreviated. Parents should do this regularly so that children are aware that they are being watched.

For example, if your child is on a computer, watch to see if he or she turns the monitor off as soon as you enter the room. The child may say it "froze" or he is trying to see if the picture will be better if it is given a rest. If a computer freezes, turning off the monitor is not the solution. The computer box would have to be turned off. They may also lessen the brightness on the monitor of a laptop. Parents should turn on the monitor or brighten the screen immediately to see what the child may be hiding regarding their activity.

Parents have complained that they do not want to monitor their children's computer usage because they believe they are "prying" into the personal lives of their children. Please realize that:

Privacy should have no boundaries when child protection is necessary.

Your child or youth could be complaining about protecting their privacy for a variety of reasons:

Your child has been engaging in producing child pornography through self-exploitation using devices you own;

Your child has been bullied because of their "personal or private" pictures that have been circulated at school and on the Internet;

Your child has arranged for a private meeting with an "unknown" they have been chatting with online;

And on it goes…

Children or youth may try to intimidate their parents or caregivers. They love to brag about what they know on devices. The knowledge of children and youth, quite often, is very limited. Their knowledge includes how to play games, text, post, engage in social media, and send emails with attachments. Knowledge related to how the computer operates or about programming is often limited.

Often, children and youth will say they are gamers and are the best. At meetings with youthful participants, these youth will brag about their extensive knowledge about texting. Never allow this type of braggadocio to intimidate you as an adult. People who are quiet about their knowledge on computers and digital devices are usually the ones who actually do know what they are doing.

Youth, especially, love to make comments about their computer and Internet "knowledge" to intimidate the listeners, particularly adults in authority or caregivers. A wise colleague in conversation with me, once said, "Never forget your rights as a parent." Intimidation should never allow you to feel inadequate as a parent – your right to discipline and guide your children should prevail. Children have a right to be reasonably disciplined. Reasonable discipline should never be viewed as abuse; children need to be prepared for society as they mature and enter their adult lives.

CHAPTER 14

CELL PHONES

Parents will share that their child loans their phone to friends to call home and other friends.

Many people leave their cell phones unattended, and loan them to other people for use. Children do this as well.

Children and youth should be cautioned about leaving their phones anywhere. Some parents have shared with me that a "friend" of their child asked to borrow their cell phone. The "friend" then completed a drug deal using a coded conversation. Or, a friend might text harassing messages to a peer using the borrowed cell phone. The activities might seem quite benign to the lending friend because the child listened to the call or witnessed texting. Little did they know their phone was being used in a way that would be incriminating for them.

Regarding the drug deal described previously, the owner of the phone witnessed the "friend" simply saying they would meet them in the parking lot at the park two blocks down at about 3:00 and then go for a coffee. She did not realize that the arrangement was to pick up some ordered street drugs. Even though the phone was loaned to an individual to make a drug exchange, there were no charges laid to the owner of the phone, but a recommendation by police was given to the parents and family to exercise more caution. Understand that sometimes information may be given that could be incriminating, even though the message seems benign to any type of illegal activity.

A cell phone should be shared as much as you would share your toothbrush, which, in most likelihood, would be not at all. If someone wants to make a call and needs a phone, YOU should be dialing the number and speaking with the person at the other end.

Yes, there are people you can trust, and judgment needs to be made in this regard. Many people have had their children, family members, or themselves subjected to criminal behaviour by people they thought they could trust. Their children have been used for activities, pictures, and videos of a criminal nature, by people the entire family trusts. Unfortunately, this type of victimization is sinister and always a secret. We cannot blame ourselves when victimization occurs. We can have all safeguards in place, but we may still fall prey to predators or dishonest people.

If a cell phone or iPad has been loaned, the contents should always be reviewed to ensure that nothing has been put on the device that could be of a criminal nature. As long as it is in your possession, always remember it is your responsibility. The owner of the device is legally responsible for the contents and activity of the device, regardless of who uses it. The legalities come back to the owner.

CHAPTER 15

NUDES

Children and youth loan their phones freely to friends or unknown persons, which can cause an unsafe situation. This is regularly done in a school setting.

Child pornography is neither an accident nor a game. It is a crime. The Canadian Criminal Code is very clear: anyone under the age of 18 is considered a child in Canada. Therefore, any pictures of nude children and, or of a sexually exploitive nature, may be interpreted as child pornography by law enforcement.

There are thousands of "nudes" in circulation on cell phones and on other devices. School Superintendents, Principals and teachers are aware of the self-exploitation of youth being in epidemic proportions. Because of today's mobile technology and the Internet, the self exploitation activity has a proliferation of which they have never seen before in their careers.

Children and youth need to realize that child pornography is not just a morality or censorship issue. It is criminal and falls under the Criminal Code. Charges can be laid related to producing, possessing and distributing child pornography, and have been laid even though youth believe they are immune because of their age. In some cases, the Youth Criminal Justice Act has been applied. In other cases, youth have been tried in adult court. Some of the investigations have taken place in the school system. Youth believe they are untouchable if it happens in a school setting. This attitude is being challenged by law enforcement.

Many students have regrets regarding their self-exploitive conduct. They realize, too late, that their pictures will be in cyber space forever. As stated by Detective Constable Jeremy Spence, "(The picture) is out there forever. It's not coming back. The Internet houses everything. The Internet does not forget."

Relationships for teens and children can change many times before they graduate from high school and after graduation. All children need to be educated regarding relationships, usual lack of longevity, and the vulnerable nature of their relationships. Too often, a partner in a relationship agrees to share a nude or intimate picture with their partner because they believe they are "in love" and it will "last forever". This illusion is often shattered and the picture is in the hands of a former partner.

Parents need to educate their children regarding "love" relationships in school. Children and youth need to be very careful about sharing their activities, information, or images, both in person and digitally. Digital data will outlast personal relationships. In other words, "The Internet does not forget." (Spence)

If a child, youth, parent, caregiver, or professional is aware of a location of an embarrassing, humiliating or harassing picture, they are able to go to the website "www.needhelpnow.ca". The website has counselors who can assist a family or youth individually, related to the needed emotional care when this occurs. The personnel on the website can also help to remove the unwanted picture from a specific location online. For example, if the picture is on a specific social media site, they will assist in removal. However, if the picture has been shared with many people and is on the Internet in unknown locations, this becomes an impossible task. The best decision is to never share a self-exploitive picture.

It is important to provide here some statistics about children/youth that should be shared with them to emphasize the degree to which intimate pictures are shared. These statistics are based on data related to a school environment:

1 in 5 teens admit to having posted a sexually suggestive or explicit photo;

1 in 3 boys report receiving an image meant for someone else;

1 in 2 teens have received a sexually suggestive image for someone else;

A photo, when sent out over today's technology, with today's apps, can reach 1,000 students in an hour.

(Bradfordtimes.ca)

Students should think very carefully before sharing ANY picture of a potentially embarrassing nature. Parents, caregivers and professionals need to explain these statistics and educate their children about the consequences and possible legal charges that could be laid against children and youth who are offenders.

CHAPTER 16

PORNOGRAPHY SITES

Some children as young as five years of age have been on pornography sites. Parents find this disturbing and do not understand how the children got to the sites. They require more knowledge to understand this issue and how to avoid it.

Following arrests of teens for sexting, a sheriff in the United States has cautioned parents about the activities of their children on digital devices. They can fall prey to criminals who are everywhere and will not stop until they find a victim. They are often people who are trusted by the family. There are even more who are unknown to the family and online.

Children and youth can create applications on computers and devices that conceal the actual application that is being used. This is effective when hiding their activities. One group of teens concealed their sexting group with the icon of a calculator. By pressing on the calculator, they had an instant link to their sexting group.

Children and youth are baited by criminals in many ways. One concept of grooming is to take a child to porn sites. A child might be playing an online game, and suddenly adult nudes or sexual activity is on the screen. This can be the first stage in grooming a child to comply with requests of a predator. This stage of grooming is used to encourage the child into thinking it is normal and acceptable to view these pictures and to engage in this type of activity.

Predators seek victims in many venues. The most popular are children's gaming sites, but they also go to social media sites. They chat, try to locate a lonely, vulnerable child and may begin to gain the trust of that child. Predators commonly use the grooming methods cited in Chapter 12. For children who can't read, verbal chats are used. Rest assured, all children's online games are potential targets of predators.

Good parents do not want their child to view pornography. When a child is taken to sites by predators grooming them with these pictures, it is too late to preserve their innocence. Once it is gone, it can never be retrieved.

As children get older, the predators go on the chats for online games and begin playing the game with the child. Of course, they pretend they are the age of the child. They do everything to earn their trust. For example, if a child says their parents are being mean to them and not letting them go to the park to play with their friends, the predator will agree with them and say their parents are the same way. Oh, by the way, which park do you like to play in the most? A predator could ask questions seeking information about the child, and say they live in a distant city. The predator could very well live down the street from the child.

Grooming can include complimenting the child on their gaming abilities. A predator can ask the child to smile for the webcam on the computer because they can see them. There is a possibility that they can be seen through the webcam if security is not set up properly on the computer. Setting security options are often missed.

There are ways for predators to use the webcam, for example, without anyone knowing. They can use it to tape unsuspecting users and their activities in front of the computer. Any business, any bedroom, any building, any church, any mosque, etc. can be targeted.

In Toronto, a couple was watching a movie on Netflix. They became intimate and did not realize that a hacker was taping them while in bed. The next day, the same hacker sent the couple the video of their night. The couple was horrified.

As stated previously, cover the webcam unless it is in use, to avoid this type of victimization.

It is even more advisable to ensure that malware is not on the machine that can open up the webcam to hackers. "BlackShades RAT" is the common malware used for this purpose. According to the FBI, the BlackShades RAT has been sold to several thousand users online since 2010. It is estimated that over a half million computers have been infected with this malware.

What would a hacker do with this software?

Once installed, a RAT provides a hacker control over the device the software is on. It usually includes the hacker having control over: files on the computer (viewing and accessing); mouse; the screen; and even record keystrokes. This would give them access to personal information and passwords. RATs can also provide access to the webcam of a device. They can secretly record video or take photos without the owner knowing it is being done. This was the case with the couple in Toronto.

A RAT program, which is a type of malware, can be purchased for under $50. Be very careful because all of your files can be hacked. A good anti-virus software would detect malware.

If you do not know how to do this, it is important to hire a computer specialist to do this for you. Make sure you have your wi-fi secured, with a good, secure password that would be difficult to hack.

Miss Teen USA winner, Cassidy Wolf, was victim to a RAT on her machine. She had a stalker who managed to install the Blackshades RAT on her laptop. He took pictures of her nude using the webcam on her device.

This type of invasion of privacy can happen to children without a RAT on the machine. Parents in Southwestern Ontario discovered their nine-year-old daughter had been sending pictures to a couple over the Internet, using the family webcam. Over a period of time, the predator couple had groomed the child to engage in self-exploitive activity by providing nudes. Had these parents been practicing digital supervision, this situation would never have reached such a level of victimization. What a tragedy that a nine-year-old had been used for this purpose. She would have been too naïve and trusting to realize the far-reaching negative consequences for such actions.

Parents of children under the age of 18 are interviewed by police or other authorities in this type of case to question what child protection methods could have been used with the child – what can now be done to ensure that your child will not engage in such acts? These types of situations are very difficult, obviously, and one everyone would want to avoid.

CHAPTER 17

HUSBANDS AND WIVES

Some spouses have found child pornography on the home computer. They realize that their spouses are guilty of putting the pictures or videos on the machine. This is problematic if the children use the same machine. Many wives have stated they do not know what to do and wondered if it was true that the material got on the machine by mistake. An understanding of the child pornography industry is necessary if adults are to deal with this type of situation.

Some wives have contacted me to talk about their home situation and to obtain advice. It was very difficult for the wives to share this information. They were frightened they could be charged for possession of child pornography. The pictures or videos were on their home computer, which was shared within their family, including their children. They were furious their children might have seen the pictures and videos. My advice and guidance to anyone calling with this type of problem, is to call the police. The police are the only people who should deal with this crime.

If someone finds child pornography material on their home computer, and the person in the household who is guilty of downloading the material says they are investigating predators, it is a very lame excuse. They use the façade that they are helping the police. A rock star in Britain used this excuse when police charged him with child pornography possession. It is an excuse given in an attempt to cover up criminal activity.

Law enforcement personnel (in Canada) would never investigate child pornography on their personal, home computers. They could be found guilty of possession and searching child pornography, all of which is a crime in Canada (see Criminal Code in the Appendices).

If anyone calls a police force to report about child pornography activity, they are treated very seriously. Anyone who is aware of child pornography should report the situation to the police.

To go further, parents, caregivers and professionals need to be aware of the "Deep" or "Dark" Web in order to fully realize the need for digital supervision in such cases. There is an underground Internet, referred to as the "Deep" web or the "Dark" web. When on a search engine using the Dark web browser, the IP address is not indexed by the search engine. To be in the Dark web, it requires a special browser for access. The Dark web is a peer-to-peer network known only to the participants. Users may refer to it as "onionland", which is a reference to the file extension of "onion".

Anyone in this section of the Internet is usually not there for positive purposes. The "Tor browser" can be used for many reasons if a person wishes to remain anonymous. The IP address of a machine is blocked from searches from law enforcement or anyone who might want to search the origin of online activity. The type of crimes being committed in the Dark Web, are not described in this book; it would be too extensive. A number of predators use the dark web to protect their criminal actions. If someone in your family or a child or youth is using Tor or a similar browser that protects anonymity, he or she should be investigated further. Parents, caregivers and professionals need to be aware and act accordingly. Ensure your digital supervision includes review of your devices and types of browsers installed. If authorities need to be notified, be sure to exercise your rights as adults and do so.

CHAPTER 18

PORN ADDICTION

Therapists have stated that youth and some children are addicted to viewing pornography online. This type of addiction can lead to curiosities of child pornography and contribution to the child pornography industry through self-exploitation and sharing of pictures that are of a self-exploitive nature with peers. Some male youth are so addicted to viewing pornography that they experience erectile dysfunction. Through digital supervision, this type of activity should be avoided.

Porn addiction is a very real problem, and growing.

When people are addicted to pornography, they find having sex with real people becomes boring and not stimulating. Young men at the age of 15 or 16 have called therapists and said they can't perform with their girlfriends any more because they find them boring. In reality, people without pornography in their lives, do not have the type of sexual performance that is fiction and staged in pictures and videos. Internet porn addiction may lead to other types of pornography, including child pornography.

A former porn star, (S. L.), from California, shared the same stage with me when I was speaking in London, Ontario in 2015. She gave horrific details about the experiences of porn stars when she was in the industry.

Many people think being a porn star is a choice. For a few, it may be a choice; however, for most, it becomes a form of income during very difficult situations in life. This was the case for S. L. and most of her colleagues in the porn industry.

She described being forced to do things sexually, getting sick with sexually transmitted diseases, experiencing assaults when she couldn't perform in front of the camera – the list is endless.

She advises everyone to stop looking at pornography in general. Continuing to view porn images only supports the porn industry. Most participants in the porn movies and pictures would make other choices if they could.

People looking at pornography need to realize the magnitude of the abuse that may have been used to create the product. With addicts to porn, the abuse is never a consideration. A porn addiction is considered an addiction within the mental health circles. This addiction can lead to many other troublesome behaviours. As in all addictions, the addicted individual will do anything to fulfill their addiction.

The story from S. L. about her endurance as a porn star was disturbing. She stated it was bad enough to be an adult in such a traumatic situation but to be a child and to be sexually exploited, was disgusting. She spoke about the terrible atrocities she had endured when being pimped out for movies and pictures. In conversation with me, she stated, "I can't imagine being a helpless child at the hands of someone using them for pictures and twisted sexual gratification. They have endured what I have, and they are innocent little children."

One therapist interviewed, who specializes in porn addiction, stated that he treats pornography addicts every day. A pornography addiction is not a crime, as long as the addict is over the age of 16 in Canada (see Canadian Criminal code). However, it is a crime when children are involved and it is defined as child pornography. He, too, spoke at the same event with S. L. and me. He was disgusted that children as young as infants were being used for the crime of child pornography.

He explained that all people who are addicted to porn need to seek counseling to stop looking at the pictures or videos. Usually, men can face erectile dysfunction as a result of being addicted to porn. Erectile dysfunction has been experienced by youth as well.

Women are not immune to this type of addiction either, but are less likely to admit to the addiction. This addiction can affect their intimacy and lives in general. Women can feel great despair and loneliness. Many addicts can begin the addiction as early as 11 years of age.

Pornography addiction can be described as an addiction that the addict cannot control regarding viewing pornography. They will continue with the addiction in spite of negative consequences in their personal lives, including social and financial issues. They will feed the addiction in spite of potential loss of their jobs, families and other important factors in their lives. The addiction to pornography, can lead into viewing child pornography.

Parents need to realize this type of addiction can begin very early. If children or youth are on porn sites, and parents are aware of the times their child is on these sites, they need to make a determination as to whether there is an addiction; or, have the child see a professional to help them deal with the addiction.

Digital supervision should include adult awareness of pornography on devices. Methods of digital supervision for acquiring this type of data are outlined later. This type of addiction can lead to other disturbing behaviours, if the child wishes to enact some of the fantasies they experience as they view porn. Blocking pornography sites is an option, however, as the child grows older, they can find ways around blocks.

CHAPTER 19

CHILD PORNOGRAPHY PRODUCTION AND DISTRIBUTION

Police have stated that children as young as eight years of age are producing, distributing and in possession of child pornography.

Children as young as eight are engaging in these types of acts. Following the previous chapter, if a child has been exposed to pornography early or if they are addicted to it, different behaviours can occur.

Siblings or peers may be used or they may be engaging in self-exploitation. Imagine being a parent or caregiver, and discovering your eight-year-old child is producing child pornography. They may have been using friends, a younger sibling, a relative or sexually exploiting themselves. At such a young age, the devices used have been purchased by the parents or caregivers for them.

One step towards protecting children includes purchasing a keylogger for computers, iPads, cell phones and any other electronic cellular device. A keylogger records every keystroke on a device. A keystroke means that any key depressed on a device is recorded in a file. Parents would learn so much about the activities of their children through the keylogger records. A more comprehensive keylogger will record all activity on any device, including screen captures, pictures, - all activity.

Younger people use popular social messaging applications marketed to teens, even though the age restriction is set at 13 or over. The text, sext, video or picture is supposed to disappear after a few seconds. However, there are third party applications that can be used to keep the data being shared, without it being erased within seconds. Screen capture can be used as well to keep pictures. (commonsensemedia.org)

This doesn't deter youth from possibly sharing inappropriate content nor being sent such content. Snapchat is just one of many apps available that offer this type of transmission of data.

If parents/caregivers have a keylogger on their devices, all keystrokes would be recorded and texting or sexting would be recorded for reference. In most keylogger environments, the recorded keystrokes can be sent to a file in the iCloud or in an environment related to the keylogger software purchased, outside of the computer hard drive. It is then not accessible to children. It can also be recorded on a hidden file on the computer; however, as children become more knowledgeable in operating computers, they may locate the file.

This type of recording is invaluable for parents when trying to practice digital supervision because the keylogger is accurate and gives a full account of communications. Some Keyloggers do not record pictures. The more comprehensive keyloggers will record all activity on the device.

There were 10 boys in Laval, Quebec, ages 13 to 15, who were arrested for sharing nudes of their girlfriends. They were using Snapchat. The boys told the girls that because it was Snapchat, the pictures would be gone immediately. Therefore, the girls complied. They had multiple poses. Unfortunately, the boys had kept the pictures using screen capture. Therefore, the pictures did not disappear as the girls believed they would.

The boys were sharing the pictures with friends, and extended the share to people in the United States. When the police became involved, arrests were made. The girls were within the same age range as the boys and, therefore, the pictures were defined as child pornography. It was a very difficult situation for the parents as well as for the girls who were victimized. For the victims, their sense of trust and friendship was totally violated. By sharing the pictures, they were engaging in a type of cyber bullying. People they trusted victimized the girls. The boys learned their behaviour was not a joke. Children and youth need to realize the extent of possible consequences for their actions. (Global News.ca)

In 2015, it became illegal in Canada to share an intimate picture without the consent of the participants. It is good that this law (Bill C-13) was passed, considering the extent of this crime in 2013.

Had the parents been using a keylogger on the cell phones, and reviewed them regularly, they would have realized that pictures were being sent using a device for which they paid, and perhaps questioned their children about it. Online sharing renders parenting a whole new issue of responsibility.

CHAPTER 20

YOUTH AND NUDES

Youth have stated that most students or friends have nudes on their cell phones. As it is common, they see nothing wrong with it.

Youth have stated that they take pictures of their genitalia, or breasts regularly and distribute them to their electronic followers and friends.

What comes to mind here is the old statement – "if your friend told you to jump off a cliff, would you do it?"

It is important that parents, caregivers, and professionals listen to what educators and police are telling them. The cases listed below will help to emphasize consequences that can result from self-exploitive activity.

Self-exploitation is more of an issue with girls. Males can engage in self-exploitation, but it is more prevalent with females. Often, when a relationship is terminated, one of the partners might engage in revenge porn by using the self-exploitive pictures. The pictures are circulated to many friends, and in some cases, a large part of a student population.

When a 17-year-old girl discovered nudes of her boyfriends ex girlfriend on his phone, she engaged in revenge porn. She sent the pictures to various friends and on social media. She had an anger issue toward the former girlfriend. This is defined as a revenge porn incident. She was convicted of possession of child pornography, distribution and uttering threats. She was charged because the picture was of a girl who was 17 years of age. (NY Daily News.com)

Self-exploitation, as an activity on its own without a relationship, can cause other issues. For example, a "sexting" group of teens kept exchanging pictures. They were sexting nudes and are, by law, considered children because they were all under the age of 18. The extent of the sharing was across several states. This occurred in North Carolina and their criminal code defines anyone under the age of 18 as a child. Even though children, they were tried as adults. Sexting can hurt so many people. In some cases, the sexting group was disguised on the device as a calculator. This would be a benign icon that a parent would not think to investigate.

The message from police to parents and caregivers is to be aware of what your children are doing on devices. If you pay for the device, the police could be knocking on your door with questions, which would be disconcerting as a parent.

Too many parents and caregivers have little knowledge of this possibility. If the parents or caregivers provide the cell phone or other device, they have a responsibility for the activity on the device.

Another example of a crime resulting from self-exploitation activities, involved young boys in Kamloops, B.C. who were charged with possessing and distributing child pornography. The investigation was conducted within the Kamloops school district. This type of investigation is very troublesome for all education staff because they could be implicated if the child is within their purview at the time of the action. The boys were charged under the Youth Criminal Justice Act. (News, CBC)

Youth need to realize they are not immune to the law just because they are conducting their crimes in a school setting. By sharing their pictures, they are contributing to the child pornography industry and are no better than the predators who are assaulting children and sharing pictures and videos.

There have been many families traumatized by the crime of child pornography and sexual assault.

In another case of revenge porn, another situation involved a Brantford, Ontario teen who was charged with distributing an intimate image without consent. He was accused of forwarding to others an image of a teenage girl in Brantford via cell phone. Both the girl and the boy were under the age of 18. (News Brantford,Brant)

Youth view cyber sexting and sharing intimate content as funny and a hoax. Girls are contributing to the galleries of the boys, thinking it is a "riot" that their pictures will be circulated everywhere. Unfortunately, when a girl or boy realizes that their picture has been circulated, they become depressed because of the social isolation that can occur. This is difficult because depression can lead to self-destructive behaviours.

Youth (girls and boys) often use nudes as a form of flirting, rather than just smiling or winking. Parents, caregivers and professionals need to realize this activity is contributing to the child pornography industry, a multi billion-dollar industry – profit that is being realized by criminals, not victims.

The behaviour of sharing intimate content is contributing to a growing disregard for humanity, which is becoming epidemic in our society. People are treating users of devices as though they are robots without feelings. We all need to take back our sense of humanity and realize that human beings are operating the Internet and devices. Parents need to teach humanity through supervision of their children and communication with them. What are positive traits of humanity - the human feelings of compassion, kindness, caring, empathy, sympathy, pride, etc. These feelings are our positive feelings for each other.

CHAPTER 21

LIABILITIES

Children as young as seven have taken pictures of their genitalia and breasts and these images are on the computers, iPads and cell phones owned by their parents.

Children and youth have stated they communicate with absolute unknown persons through social media.

When taking pictures on a device that is actually owned by their parents, children unknowingly participate in being part of a bigger issue. If the children have engaged in self-exploitation, the parents are then in possession of illegal content - pictures, video, audio, or written content. If the authorities find illegal content on the parents' devices, they can then investigate the parents for possession. In fact, after interviewing some police officers, they shared that they would contact a child protection services agency to report a situation if children are engaged in producing, sharing or distributing child pornography. They would do this to protect the children.

Parents are advised to check the devices used by their children regularly, and at random times. Have cell phones turned in at a certain time daily or at random times. If children and youth have data on the phone, and the phone is not turned in, they could visit various sites throughout the night or conducting other potentially illegal activities.

Professionals should realize that a child under their care and supervision is their responsibility, which includes the digital activities of the child. It is important that guidance and supervision be diligent. If there is a situation with a child arranging to meet someone outside of their home or other facility, the times of the chats or emails are recorded within the cell phone records. Through investigation of the phone records, it is determined who was supervising the child at the time the chats and other activities took place. The adult responsible for the supervision of the child is then in a situation where they are questioned. There can be liability on the part of the adult.

I had an unfortunate experience in 1998. Chats were becoming a new item on the Internet. Students were using them all of the time. I told the students to be careful while on the Internet and not to engage in chats. If I found students chatting, I always asked them to stop. It needs to be emphasized that with this was a new activity. Very little was known about liabilities and possible situations for victimization related to chatting.

After about four months, I had the Principal at my classroom door asking me if I taught "Julie." I responded with "yes". The Principal said that the student lived in a group home and was not entitled to Internet privileges. She then proceeded to tell me that a man had called the group home looking for "Julie." The man was about 45 years of age. The staff at the group home told the Principal the only way the student could have met the man was online. "Julie" told them that she had been chatting in my classroom.

The Principal was very supportive and stated that it is a new activity on the Internet and that she didn't really blame me for it. However, she also stated that more vigilance was required when students were using the computers and being online.

This taught me a lesson I will never forget. Firstly, that a child could have been abducted, or worse. I was very upset about that. After I thought about it, I realized my entire career could have been in question.

From that incident on, I was hyper-vigilant regarding online activity in my classroom. I did not sit down while students were engaged on computers. I did not allow any social media or chats. My classroom was more disciplined than ever before.

This experience taught me that one couldn't be too careful with students and children. In that I was the Network Administrator, I was always telling colleagues to police their classrooms with vigilance and not allow online games, chats, or social media in the classroom. Unfortunately, colleagues thought I was too strict and should "chill out".

Children and youth need to realize that having multiple "friends" (some brag they have 2,200 and more) is unsafe. They also need to realize that when they have friends, they are connected with all of the friends of their friends. Very few people truly know their friends online; most are merely known by association, and have never met in person. How many people, out of 2,200, do you truly know? Within the 2,200 friends, the chances are there would be at least one who could end up causing a child difficulties, grief, or victimization. Children tend to share personal data they shouldn't, which puts them at risk.

With digital supervision, parents need to differentiate digital friendships versus "actual" friendships as the children operate with digital devices. The definition of "friend" must be explained.

CHAPTER 22

PRIVACY OF CHILDREN AND YOUTH

Youth and children have stated that they prefer the social media sites that offer texting and other communications, which claim to provide anonymity. They believe their parents and caregivers will never know about their chats, nor confront them about them, nor realize that any images or content can be viewed, saved or recorded by others.

Parents are afraid to invade the privacy of the activities of their children.

Parents have asked how they can monitor the activities of their children without invading their privacy. Parents need to realize that their OWN activities on the Internet, particularly specific social media sites, can cause privacy issues for their children, themselves, and their families. Too often, what parents post, innocently, is personal information about their children. When a child is younger than eight years of age, this is a poor choice because of the following scenarios:

A parent has a picture of their child at their house or at the front door of the school, with the name of the school displayed prominently.

A mother posts all of her pictures and her comments in social media for all to see. She might have about 550 friends on her site. She has unknowns as well because she thinks having lots of "friends" signi-fies her popularity. She is a young mother, 28, and believes she is so much more computer literate than her friends and children. After all, why shouldn't she post pictures of her children daily on social media – everyone else is doing it and it means she is a good, caring mother, right? She even posts pictures of what her children have for breakfast every day. Then, all of her friends will know what an excellent mother she is. This parent has little regard for the privacy of her children. It would be better if she kept her information private for the safety of the children.

This parent is suffering from social media pressure and excessive engagement. She believes that social media is keeping her from being lonely, and by telling everyone what an excellent person and parent she is she feels more worthy. She feels pressure from friends who might have more pictures of their children on social media sites than she does. Competition is prevalent on social media.

This parent has told everyone, including unknowns, the following infor-mation that a predator can use against their children, and ultimately, against the entire family.

The names of the children;

The pictures of the children;

A picture of their house;

Described anxiety of their children;

Given names of friends of their children and their mothers' names;

A picture of the school.

What the children have for breakfast;

Friend's names.

All of the above information and more can be used to embarrass children or put children at risk. Parents, like anyone else, are known to post personal information, such as their real birth dates, the birth dates and/or ages of their children, their real address, their place of employment, their marital status, their marital issues, their religious/political beliefs, holiday trip information, personal purchases, work issues, etc.

Please – many parents have talked about their children and the safety of their children. Social media awareness for parents is of paramount importance in initially negating any danger for children.

There are videos on YouTube that teach people how to "crack" codes on social media sites. Many people have said that their social media is "tight" and that "no one" can get on their site. Even the Pentagon in the United States has difficulty keeping terrorists and criminals off their servers.

There are government agencies, in Canada and the United States that have developed Critical Infrastructure Protection (CIP) policies to protect from infrastructure attack. In Canada, the government has developed partnerships with various corporations to help eliminate vulnerabilities related to cyber attacks that would damage or invade critical infrastructure.

Realize that social media is "Mickey Mouse" in having security features that prevent privacy breaches by hackers, including predators. The security on social media can be penetrated if someone really wants to do so. The managers of social media sites may change security parameters at times, increasing or decreasing those parameters, without users being notified. When using a service, such as an application that has been downloaded for free, your personal information is not necessarily protected. There is no legal obligation on the part of the application developer to keep all users informed of changes. They may give notices but many users fail to read them or understand them.

Parents who worry about invading the privacy of their children are a problematic situation. Before cell phones were common (and we are talking since the year 2000), parents were more informed about the activities of their children. Chats and computers were just becoming common. Cell phones were not used by all people.

There were no iPads, and so on.

When a child received a telephone call on a landline, families usually knew who was calling and could give guidance to their children regarding their activities. Now many parents are remote from the social lives of their children, which is alarming. They never know who is communicating with their children on cellphone, email nor by texts. Even though some parents pay for the cell phone, some never access the cell phone bill to review the call history of their children.

With social media apps and various activities of children on computers and digital devices, parents should purchase a keylogger for the cell phones of their children. The keylogger can also be put on a laptop, iPad, computer and the like.

My advice is to "email" pictures to relatives and friends you know. It is an "old fashioned" way of sharing but you will then know that only your relatives and friends are receiving pictures of your family. The recipients of such emails are appreciative of the personal approach to sharing of the pictures or videos. This type of behaviour is part of digital supervision. Parents are sharing through email and setting an example for their children.

CHAPTER 23

SELFIES AND SELF-EXPLOITATION

The self-exploitation of children and youth is becoming a growing concern. This is becoming more known as 'sexting' among children and youth. Sexting is defined as, an individual (including children and youth) creating, sending or sharing sexual images and/or videos with friends or peers through the use of the Internet and/or electronic devices. This self-exploitation is is referred to as "taking a selfie".

SOME STATISTICS:

22% of teen girls have admitted to sending sexts;

18% of teen boys have admitted to sending sexts.

18% of boys have admitted to sending sexts.

Of the 70% of teen girls who have sexted, 61% have said that they did so because they were pressured.

24% of high school aged students (between the ages of 14 and 17) (nobullying.com)

The issue in the above-noted statistics should be obvious. Number one, these are statistics of teens who have "admitted" to engaging in sexting. The other, is girls have felt pressured into doing it by boyfriends or peers. Boys do not feel the same amount of pressure to do so. Digital supervision, in this type of situation, must incorporate the education of girls and boys regarding pressure by peers to create and share selfies. Refusal techniques need to be identified and discussed. The statistics point to boys pressuring girls more than the reverse.

There is a tremendous amount of pressure within the social circles of teenagers related to selfies. The resulting behaviours of peers when this type of situation occurs can be debilitating for the teen who has engaged in self-exploitation. They can feel isolation and remote from all activities of their peers.

If the selfie is nude or a partial nude and of a teen under the age of 18, it can be interpreted as child pornography. Parents and caregivers, as part of digital supervision need to further explain to their children the issues regarding the Canadian Criminal Code and how children can be charged for creating and distributing child pornography through their actions.

To add to the concept of selfies even further, the American Mental Health Association has added selfies as a mental health addiction. If the selfie activity is done daily and regularly, and a person has their everyday activities interrupted because of the activity, it is considered an addiction.

A 19-year-old teen, Danny in England was addicted to taking selfies when he was 15. He was known to have taken at least 200 selfies per day. He was considered obsessive compulsive and kept taking the selfies to create a 'perfect' selfie. He became so obsessed with taking them, he attempted to commit suicide when he just could not create the 'perfect' selfie. He dropped out of school and spent nearly ten hours per day taking selfies in an attempt to create a 'perfect' one.

Danny's case has been described as being extreme. To paraphrase a Psychiatrist, Dr. David Veale, who has explained it is not a vanity issue but a mental health issue. Suicide is a threat in this type of addiction. (Addiction.com)

Digital supervision should include monitoring children to ensure that excessive selfies or addictions do not exist. Parents should continually communicate with their children about the harms of selfies and excessive application of the harmful exercise. The self-exploitation issue should be part of the discussion as well.

CHAPTER 24

PREDATOR DIGITAL EXPERTISE

Child abductors are known to frequent playgrounds, parks, pools, youth organizations, scouts, girl guides, karate schools, neighbourhood gatherings, family gatherings, sports teams, sports events, arenas, religious buildings/organizations, malls, stores, and grocery stores – get the picture? They are everywhere.

Many people have asked if this is "just a third world issue". Child pornography is very much in Canada and is everywhere. It is in our homes, our schools, and our churches, EVERYWHERE.

To review the history of computer development:

Electronic computer devices were developed in the 1950's in the United States, France and the United Kingdom.

Tim Paterson, of Seattle Computer Products, developed 86-DOS.

Microsoft purchased DOS from Tim Paterson for $75,000.

In 1980, Microsoft began to market 86-DOS to manufacturers and eventually renamed it "MS-DOS".

Steve Wozniak and Steve Jobs co-founded "Apple" in 1976 and started to sell Wozniak's Apple 1 personal computer system.

The United States Department of Defense developed ARPANET, a network that was IP based.

In 1982 the standard TCP/IP network was developed. I have managed networks that were TCP/IP based.

(Wikipedia.com)

With these devices being developed in North America, it is perplexing that anyone would believe the crime of child pornography to be non-existent in North America. The very devices being used for the purpose were developed in North America.

Too often, parents are nervous of their child being targeted by abductors or being abused in some way, sexually or otherwise. They often take their children to school with great traffic risk, wait for buses, and pick their children up. There is an inherent fear in parents that their children might be harmed, and rightly so.

Children are at risk in many situations, however, adults need to realize that children are at great risk online. Children are being targeted and abducted via online chats, gaming, social media and others. This is a new definition of abduction. They may not be physically "abducted," but they are being targeted while on games, chats and social media. Children are being channeled off to undesirable xxx sites on the Internet, which they would not choose themselves. Do they tell their parents? Very rarely and highly unlikely. They usually know what they have seen may be "wrong" and do not share with their parents for fear of being in trouble.

Also, what most adults do not know, is that people who want to engage in criminal behaviour drive around cities to find unsecure routers. They will log on to an unsecure router and conduct their activities undetected. They will download massive amounts of child pornography and leave. The homeowner is then suspected of being engaged in this activity.

Predators may be going on your laptop webcams and viewing what is going on in your home because they can hack in. They are going on online baby monitors and viewing what is going on with parents caring for their babies because, again, they can access these devices remotely.

There was a case in Southwestern Ontario. Parents had an online baby monitor. A hacker started talking to the father that he could see who feeding his child while rocking in a rocking chair. This was very frightening for the parents. Advice here – never have a baby monitor that is managed online. Yes, passwords can be used; however, good hackers can hack in past passwords.

Parents have worried about their child being abducted or harmed at school, on the way to school, in the playground, or on a field trip. Predators have digital expertise to target children in an online environment. They know what type of child might go along with their requests. They can find the vulnerable, shy, lonely child online, as they do in playgrounds, parks, malls, churches, and other areas.

Parents have also said many times that there children are up all night on the Internet, either playing online games or chatting. They have been at a loss as to how to deal with this situation. They are aware their children maybe communicating with undesirables in the middle of the night.

It is important to have an Internet down time in your home. Be sure the router is located in a section of your home that the children cannot access, preferably in a parental bedroom. The downtime should be the same time every night to establish a routine. Unplug the network cable, turn off the router, or program the router to shut off. Parents will then know their children are not on the Internet at night. This does not include data access on a cell phone. Be sure to have cell phones turned in at night.

Be aware of any wireless routers accessible within range of your home that may be unsecure. Your children may access the Internet through a neighbour's wireless. In this case, it is best to locate the router in your area and alert the neighbours that they need to secure their router. There have been cases where police have questioned owners of unsecure routers because criminal activity was occurring through their unsecure router.

One family had installed a new wireless router in their home. The father was having difficulty setting up a password and went to bed thinking he would complete the task the next day. While in bed, a loud knocking came at the door in the early morning hours. He went down the stairs as the knock came again.

He opened the door to several swat team police officers with guns pointed at him. They were yelling and telling him he was a pervert and they found out. The man was terrified.

He realized that he should have finished setting up the password on the router the night before. It was determined that a pedophile had been downloading child pornography using his router.

This story emphasizes the need to secure your router, whether at home or in an office. Pedophiles drive around cities to find wireless routers. They park their cars and obtain all of the pictures they want very quickly and drive off. (DailyTech).

Online games are very popular with children. Some children have recorded predators chatting with them online. Predators use these chats to sexually groom and convince children to go along with them. There are plenty of sites on the Internet that explain predator involvement with children on children's games. In order to lure a child, they will offer them electronics, trips, gifts, and other items to have the child go along with their requests.

Predators will play online games to find victims, and are also guilty of "trolling". Trolls try to antagonize players by making comments to make them angry. They also try to obtain information from players for their own selfish reasons. They will ruin a game and can get players very upset. Some younger children under the age of six have been victimized by trolls. They become very upset and have even been known to destroy the devices (iPad, computer, gaming system) because the troll did a great job antagonizing. These children are too young to under-stand what is going on.

The best way to get rid of trolls is to ignore them. Otherwise, children may react to trolls poorly by getting upset. This needs to be explained to children. Some children get so upset they destroy their devices. However, parents always need to realize that their child may be the victim and not know how to deal with trolling. Children should be instructed to leave a chat or game if there are trolls.

To all parents and caregivers, avoid allowing online games as much as possible. This is particularly true for children under the age of eight. After a certain age, peer pressure causes other relational issues. Online games seem to be necessary because children can game with friends from their own home. Remember – just because your children are home, does NOT mean they are safe. They could be playing online with several unknowns within your home who have predator intentions.

Filter software should be installed on all devices including cell phones, iPads, computers, etc. Filter software environments are used to "filter" any unwanted websites, data, etc. that you do not want your child to see. There is a setup involved and parents may need to have a computer specialist do this procedure for them. Unfortunately, as children mature, they can usually work around a filter, but it at least slows them down.

There is also a parental control feature on Windows systems. Parents can use the controls to manage access. Times for computer use, games, etc. can be set. Children can be asked for a password in order to play certain games. The parents would setup parental controls and know the passwords. These controls can also block access to certain games and sites.

For more information, access: http://windows.microsoft.com/en-ca/windows/set-parental-controls#1TC=windows-7

This type of control is good when a child is very young; however, older children will be able to get around this feature, which is why this is not discussed in detail.

From a victim of child pornography:

> "It used to be that predators used instamatic pictures to lure children to be a part of their sinister plot – these pictures did not require processing and were child pornography pictures. These pictures were used to make the potential victim believe it was "okay" to take part.
>
> They use child pornography as a steppingstone, always getting more extreme to fulfill their desires and fantasies with collection of child pornography a major issue with pedophiles who physically abuse children.
>
> Parks and public places: Predators look for "victims" – quiet, shy, loners without a confident walk and look.
>
> This is even more evident and true in the digital world, where predators do their homework, and target those online personalities that they will have success with... there is a global world out there and many possible victims from which to choose."

JAMES WILLIAMS

James has been extremely willing to help in the fight against child pornography. I am very grateful that he has consented to be quoted in this book.

CHAPTER 25

PHOTO DNA AND METADATA

You don't believe in the crimes previously stated? Read on...

A Facebook crime occurs every 40 minutes: From killings to grooming; OVER 15,000 cases are linked to the site. (DailyMail, UK).

That's just Facebook among many other online sites where people share information.

To combat criminal activity, Microsoft engineered a new software program that can assign and retrieve photo DNA from pictures. Microsoft has donated it to the National Centre For Missing and Exploited Children in the United States, a technology referred to as Photo DNA. This software environment is designed to help fight the spread of graphic child pornography online. It is hoped it will stop child pornographers from sharing their pictures.

The technology works by creating a unique signature for a digital photograph, which can be compared to a unique human finger print or to a unique human DNA. The programmed DNA for the photograph can then be used to find online copies of the worst child pornography images known. The only disadvantage to it is the photograph has to have the combination of "hash sets" attached to it to identify it, which is used for further investigation. This DNA program is used by several police forces across North America. Once the DNA is attached, police can find pictures and locate predators and hopefully, victims. There are millions of pictures within the program database.

Regarding locating the origin of pictures, if users leave the geo-location on their cell phones, iPads, cameras, movie cameras, computers, and other electronic cellular devices, the originating location of where the picture was taken, can be traced. This information is referred to as "metadata."

Metadata is basically information about other information. It is a record of how, when, and by whom particular data is collected. On a picture, metadata can provide the time it was taken, longitude and latitude regarding the location it was taken, and other information. If people have the geolocation on with the device they use for taking a picture, the metadata will include the location the picture was taken.

Child protection is one reason why most social media sites remove metadata from pictures that are uploaded. By removing metadata from pictures, it helps to remove the ability of predators and unknowns to be able to find where children or users live. Of course, if parents or children have their real address and other personal information in their social media profile, it becomes easier for a predator. It is best to have geolocation turned off on all devices, unless you really need to have metadata recorded.

Professional photographers dislike having metadata removed for uploads. The copyright on their pictures is then removed. Without copyright on their pictures, people may be able to use their pictures for free.

Email can cause issues for protection. If children, youth, or adults decide to send an email to a person that is an unknown, and who is their social media contact list, the sender is sending detailed information about where he or she lives, the ISP they are using, etc. The "header" on an email contains very revealing information as illustrated below:

Trace Email Result

At Mon, 4 Apr 2016 17:07:35 +0000 (UTC), invitations@linkedin.com sent you an email from the IP Address 108.174.6.149. View Email Owner

IP Address:	108.174.6.149
Host of this IP:	mailb-ce.linkedin.com
Organization:	LinkedIn Corporation
ISP:	LinkedIn Corporation
City:	Mountain View
Country:	United States
State:	California
Postal Code:	94043
Time zone:	America/Los_Angeles
Local Time:	04.04.2016 17:49:38

Header from my personal files

This is a very benign email header, coming from LinkedIn Corporation. Notice it contains the IP address of the sender computer, the host, the ISP, and location in the United States. Some locater software will even give you a map as to the location of the sending computer, within longitude and latitude coordinates.

If a person sends an email with a picture that includes metadata attached to it, then a predator has even more detailed information about the location of the sender, details about dates of the picture, etc. People should exercise extreme caution regarding the sharing of pictures and sending email to unknowns.

The other side of this type of issue is children and youth sharing self-exploitive pictures through email with unknowns. If a child or youth decides to email a picture containing nudity, and that picture has meta-data on it, he or she is sending location from two sources, the picture and the header of the email. This type of information is very important and should be known to all users for their own safety.

As a network administrator, I was asked to provide email header information to police to determine when an email was sent, and the location from where it was sent. What can be determined is if it was sent from a home computer, work computer or other source. The header data is helpful for law enforcement.

The greatest caution that is given with social media use and email is to always be very careful with personal information and data. Security is changed regularly in most social media environments and you may be unaware of how changes might affect your privacy information and settings. Digital Supervision should include education related to information about emails and metadata of pictures.

CHAPTER 26

CHILD REFUSAL METHODS

Parents and caregivers have stated that it is difficult to instill in children the ability an ability to refuse – to say "no". Parent by example. Teach children that saying not to adults or friends can be okay in certain circumstances.

Parents try to tell their children to say "no" to certain requests. These requests have been outlined previously in this book. Grooming is used regularly if a predator believes he has found a "target" or child who can be easily persuaded to go along with their requests.

Often, teens are groomed, and still find it difficult to understand information that is being given to them by possible predators. They participate in chats, send pictures, make arrangements to meet, etc. An unknown might ask them to send a picture because they are "beautiful." Flattery is a great source for grooming insecure, maturing youth.

In all cases, parents have to tell their children and youth to say "no" with conviction and to NOT give an explanation.

Here is an example: an unknown online says to a 10-year-old female that she is beautiful and to please send him or her a picture. The girl is lonely, has very few friends, and believes she is a "plain Jane". A predator will have realized this through chatting with the child.

The girl states, "well, no, my Dad and Mum would be very angry with me if I sent you a picture."

"Well," says the predator, "I have seen you through your webcam (whether he has or not) and I would like to have a picture from you so that I can have you in my life if you are not on the computer."

The child says, "but my parents might find out."

"Oh no, they won't find out. I am an expert in computers and they will never find out. Come on..."

The girl, through offering an explanation, has opened herself up to more grooming techniques by a predator. Peers can use these techniques as well. The begging, threatening, and the giving of ultimatums are commonly used.

Saying no without an explanation, gives little chance for an argument from a predator.

When a child is in a position of being in a room with a predator, this can become overwhelming and dangerous for the child. Refusal techniques in a person-to-person environment with a predator would be difficult. All circumstances are different – the age of the child, the environment, the relationship of the predator, and other variables. Methods of refusal or coping in this type of situation will not be discussed for obvious reasons – too many variables.

Adults, for any type of situation, often give an explanation. They say, "No, I can't go to your party because I have other plans." The adult's friend asking may have an argument against that, and try to convince their friend to attend their social gathering. "Come after your other plans are finished," and so on.

Parents need to set an example in these types of cases for their children, so they will witness the adults saying no without an explanation. This is not always the case, as sometimes it is important to save friendships by giving an explanation as to why a person cannot accept an invitation. However, periodically, not giving an explanation is a good example for children. Saying "no, thank you", is all that is needed and still be cordial. Always remember, we should parent by example.

Digital supervision should include an adult practicing actions that give an example to children.

CHAPTER 27

WEB WATCHING AND MIRRORING

For more computer literate parents and caregivers, there are software environments that allow the operator of the environment to view multiple devices. For example, a supervising adult would be able to go from a computer, to a cell phone, to a laptop, etc. and view the devices without the child knowing. In some environments, a parent or manager can view multiple devices, depending on the interface or infrastructure of the devices. Some employers do this type of action in the workplace. I have viewed other screens as a network administrator. The same type of setup on a home device would be the same as in a network situation.

In this case, the information can be stored in a web-based file for the parent to access if necessary. Parents should avoid telling children about this type of security setup. Manufacturers of software love to say their product is infallible and that children will never be able to find out or change things. In some cases, the child and youth being monitored may realize it and find some way to hack the system. This would be the unusual, computer "expert" within the youth community.

A parent can also mirror the activity of a child's cell phone to their phone. This means that the supervising parent can store the activity of their child's phone and view it later or view the activity simultaneously. This works for the younger children who are not aware that it is being done. It is invaluable when trying to protect children from predators. Mirroring is an activity that is available on most smart devices. A parent should go to the service provider of their cell phone to inquire as to the methods of mirroring for their specific device.

A parent in Toronto mirrored his 12-year-old daughter's cell phone. He was a guest speaker for a Child Pornography Hurts presentation. He realized she was texting someone and the texts were becoming sexual in nature. He printed out the texting on the child's cell phone and took it to the police.

There was an extensive investigation. The father was sure the person sexting his daughter was an unknown to the family.

After a week, the police narrowed their search to a home in Ohio. When they entered the home, the predator was drunk, sitting at a computer with multiple videos at his side as he watched a child pornography video on the computer. The father was disgusted, as were the police. The result: the arrest of the predator and investigation of the predator computer. The results of the investigation revealed a child pornography ring and the police then performed multiple arrests. The diligent activity of this parent helped to end a child pornography ring, but more importantly, save his child from a possible abduction.

Parents can install an application on children's phones that will copy to the phone of the parent. There are several available and are often referred to as iPhone Spy, Android Spy or Blackberry Spy. They can be used to effectively monitor the activity of a cell phone. The application will enable live viewing of texts, pictures, etc. The parent can also view a person the child is communicating with. Again, a tech literate parent would be required. Such an application would efficient and the person being watched would have little knowledge of the monitoring taking place.

A web interface device (Untangle is one) is a new type of device, which is interfaced with the computer and the router to "untangle" any type of unwanted Internet activity. Web filters are used in schools and can be used on home networks. On networks, this type of device may be referred to as a 'proxy' server. A proxy server monitors activity and can filter web access. This type of program can act as an extra firewall but not interfere with the firewall on the machine.

Web filter software environments can be set to filter any websites or content with which parents do not want their children engaged. Unfortunately, if the children were permitted to go on sites with chats and online games, controlling predator activity on the gaming sites would be limited.

CHAPTER 28

WHO IS ON SOCIAL MEDIA?

Child predators. They thank parents for letting their children chat with them online.

Human Traffickers. They go on holidays with the money they earn from selling unsuspecting children to pedophiles.

Home invaders. They thank your children for posting online that the family is going on vacation to Disney World.

Child Pornography Rings

Identity Theft Operations

Kidnappers

Murderers

Rapists

Witness Intimidators

Fraud

Violent Offenders

What is personal information?

Your school

Your work place

Your real name

Your real age

Your real birth date

Your real eye colour

Your grade

Your sex

Your address

Your phone number

The real names of people in your family

Post you are on holidays

Post where your parents or you work

Post your parents or your hours

Post a picture, or several pictures

Email address

Personal information about your relationships

The list is endless...

It is important to understand that all information about you should be considered personal when on the Internet, through chats, and social media. The information you share is considered data for anyone to access. Hackers and other criminals can use it to their advantage.

Consider that most criminals engage in hacking activity because that is how they acquire information they need to engage in, and be successful in, criminal behaviour related to digital data. More than one in four people claim they have been hacked. Nothing is private after it is posted for all to see.

Below are some startling statistics about the Internet and crimes against children, from www.victimsfirst.gc.ca, "The Office of the Federal Ombudsman for Victims of Crime (OFOVC)... an independent resource for victims in Canada."

Tens of thousands of new images or videos are put on the Internet every week.

Hundreds of thousands of searches for child sexual abuse images are performed daily.

Police reported overall sexual assaults in Canada declined in 2014.

Police-reported sexual violations against children continued to increase in 2014.

One of the only violent crime categories to increase in 2014 was sexual violations against children, making it one of the few increases in crime categories since 2013. This increase in sexual violations against children has been a trend within the previous four years. The data collected includes data on accessing, possessing, making, printing or distributing child pornography in Canada. The number and rate of child pornography incidents continued to rise, by 41% in 2014, over the previous year. (StatsCanada).

COMMON SCENARIO

You innocently post a picture of your six–year-old on a social media site; you say how proud you are of "John" going into grade one at Smith Elementary School; you say his best friend, Ian, is going too. You have befriended an unknown on your social media account. Or worse, you have a known person you don't realize is a person of questionable intent.

The unknown person goes to your son's school, tells him Mommy is coming, but he needs to pick him up because her car broke down. He then sells your son to a pedophile in Toronto. How innocent is the posting now?

AND

You post personal information about your family on social media – interests of your children, activities of your children, nightmares or dreams your children are having. Keep everything private about your family, especially by keeping it offline!

Information such as this can be used to abduct your children – to instill trust so that they will go with a predator. You never know what friends are truly about – who they are connected to as a friend?

True Scenario...

A woman had a sixth birthday party for her son, invited the children, and took pictures of the children in their bathing suits around the pool and posted them on a social media site. Innocent?

The police came to her door and showed her the picture of her son, nude, in a sexual position with an adult and asked if this was her son. A pedophile had morphed her picture and made it look like a child pornography photo session. The woman was suspected of being a predator. This would be a parent's worst nightmare.

The police realized the situation and explained it to her. The police told the mother they would be monitoring the situation for the family.

CHAPTER 29

DATA AND CASES

A Pennsylvania man was arrested for:

- sexually explicit images of children were discovered in his OneDrive cloud storage account and his Microsoft email account.

- Microsoft reported him after the company found the images and alerted the authorities in the United States.

Google detected a man in Houston for a similar issue. Google found child abuse images in the man's email and also reported him to the authorities. He had been convicted as a sex offender in 1994.

LANDSLIDE PRODUCTIONS

A child pornography company out of Fort Worth Texas, called Landslide had a complex network of some 5,700 websites worldwide (especially in Russia and Indonesia) that stored child pornography images. The operation in Fort Worth acted as a gateway into the network.

OPERATION CANDYMAN

Candyman was an open e-group maintained by Yahoo that was involved in exchanging child pornography images. It had 7,000 members, 4,600 of whom were in the United States and the remaining 2,400 lived around the world.

Is your child at risk?

Is your child always online whenever they can be?

Is there porn on your child's computer or cellular devices (iPhone, iPad, Android, Blackberry, tablet, etc.)?

Is your child receiving phone calls from unknowns (you don't know)? Is your child making calls to unknown numbers?

Has your child receiving gifts ? These could be gifts from someone who could be a peer or an unknown adult.

Have you found out your child has an email account that you did not know about?

Has your child become irritable and defiant with your requests?

Has your child become withdrawn from the family (which is what happened in the case of Jennie)?

Has your child told you stories about "friends" whom you believe may actually be about themselves? Often, children will relate to actual incidents about "friends."

It is always advisable to keep an open line of communication with your children so that if any of these types of situations surface, you might be able to discuss them openly with your children, and then find help if needed.

STATISTICS

30%+ of searches in eDonkey P2P network are related to child sexual abuse

42% of sextortion victims met their predators online.

THORN SEXTORTION SURVEY 2015

NCMEC reviewed 22 million images and videos of suspected child sexual abuse imagery in its victim identification program in 2013 – more than a 5,000% increase since 2007.

WEARETHORN.ORG

19% of identified offenders in a survey had images of children younger than 3 years old; 39% younger than 6 years old; and 83% younger than 12 years old.

MISSINGKIDS.ORG

CHAPTER 30

SUMMARY AND FINAL RECOMMENDATIONS

Social media can be good positive channels for communication. Many people use them worldwide. Families who are separated by miles can keep their families closer by communicating using chats, pictures, stories, and videos through the use of social media.

Most people use the Internet, social media, digital devices, computers, etc. on a daily basis. We are communicating electronically like never before in history. However, we also need to be aware of the negative channels within these communication possibilities. This book has been written to help everyone realize that child protection needs to be expanded to include digital supervision of all children.

Parents, caregivers and professionals need to realize that children and youth making poor digital choices and putting themselves in dangerous situations (both physically and emotionally) through the use of digital devices, are in epidemic numbers.

We cannot be bystanders any longer. Adults need to adopt digital supervision and apply it regularly so that children and youth in their care will be in a better position to make better choices, through the guidance and supervision of the adults.

To summarize recommendations:

Monitor the activities of children on cellular devices.

Play online games with your children, either in person or anonymously, to know and understand the child's activity, to teach the child appropriate communication skills.

Install filter software on all devices, including cell phones.

Install keyloggers on devices to record all keystrokes and activity. It should be a keylogger that does not record passwords. Malware can capture passwords recorded with keyloggers (and in other environments as well).

Have emails originated and written by your children forwarded or copied (cc'd) to parents/caregivers for monitoring.

Be sure one of the many anonymity browsers (ones which hide the IP address so that a person can operate on the Internet without detection), is not on a home computer or other device. This type of browser will bypass a filter or Net Nanny type of program on the machine.

Review all pictures and web histories on devices. Perhaps have a rule that only the parent can erase web histories.

Review any software environments to ensure that webcams, Facetime or Skype, or similar applications are not being used to create inappropriate videos. Check all video files on all devices.

Review Skype, FaceTime, Twitter activity and possible Periscope use, and/or other similar apps. Ensure there is no real-time video transmission. New apps are being created all the time.

Viewing pornography has an age limit of 16 in Canada. This is not to be confused with "child pornography". Child Pornography is any picture, video, cartoon, written story, etc. which depicts sexual involvement of a child under the age of 18, all of which is illegal. It is important to practice digital supervision to ensure that children are not viewing pornography while underage. It is also important to ensure this so that children will not develop an addiction to porn.

Through monitoring, ensure your child is not engaging in illegal hacking practices. This can be done through review of keylogger files. If children are on sites that are questionable or engaging in this type of activity, the keylogger file would give an indication. If parents are unsure of what this would mean, it is advisable to consult with a computer technician or specialist.

Turn off or unplug the network cable on your router at night. Keep your router in the parental bedroom if possible. Check for unsecure wireless routers in your area.

Exercise caution when transmitting pictures through email and social media.

Be sure geolocation is turned off on all devices (including cell phones, cameras, video cameras, computers, iPads, laptops, etc.). Turn it on only when necessary or desired.

Exercise caution when emailing unknowns. The header on the email can reveal location and more details about the origin of the email.

Know your children's passwords on ALL devices and monitor/review the devices regularly.

Teach your children that humanity must still exist and this should be respected as much online as it is in person. Humanity in this context would be the entire human race or the characteristics that belong uniquely to human beings, such as kindness, love, empathy, mercy and sympathy.

Mirror the activity of your children on their cell phones to your phone.

APPENDIX A

CANADIAN CRIMINAL CODE

Related to Child Pornography

"163.1 (1) In this section, child pornography means

(a) a photographic, film, video or other visual representation, whether or not it was made by electronic or mechanical means,

(i) that shows a person who is or is depicted as being under the age of eighteen years and is engaged in or is depicted as engaged in explicit sexual activity, or

(ii) the dominant characteristic of which is the depiction, for a sexual purpose, of a sexual organ or the anal region of a person under the age of eighteen years;

(b) any written material, visual representation or audio recording that advocates or counsels sexual activity with a person under the age of eighteen years that would be an offence under this Act;

(c) any written material whose dominant characteristic is the description, for a sexual purpose, of sexual activity with a person under the age of eighteen years that would be an offence under this Act; or

(d) any audio recording that has as its dominant characteristic the description, presentation or representation, for a sexual purpose, of sexual activity with a person under the age of eighteen years that would be an offence under this Act.

Making child pornography (2) Every person who makes, prints, publishes or possesses for the purpose of publication any child pornography is guilty of an indictable offence and liable to imprisonment for a term of not more than 14 years and to a minimum punishment of imprisonment for a term of one year.

Distribution, etc. of child pornography (3) Every person who transmits, makes available, distributes, sells, advertises, imports, exports or possesses for the purpose of transmission, making available, distribution, sale, advertising or exportation any child pornography is guilty of an indictable offence and liable to imprisonment for a term of not more than 14 years and to a minimum punishment of imprisonment for a term of one year.

Possession of child pornography (4) Every person who possesses any child pornography is guilty of

(a) an indictable offence and is liable to imprisonment for a term of not more than 10 years and to a minimum punishment of imprisonment for a term of one year; or

(b) an offence punishable on summary conviction and is liable to imprisonment for a term of not more than two years less a day and to a minimum punishment of imprisonment for a term of six months.

Accessing child pornography (4.1) Every person who accesses any child pornography is guilty of

(a) an indictable offence and is liable to imprisonment for a term of not more than 10 years and to a minimum punishment of imprisonment for a term of one year; or

(b) an offence punishable on summary conviction and is liable to imprisonment for a term of not more than two years less a day and to a minimum punishment of imprisonment for a term of six months.

Interpretation (4.2) For the purposes of subsection (4.1), a person accesses child pornography who knowingly causes child pornography to be viewed by, or transmitted to, himself or herself.

Aggravating factor (4.3) If a person is convicted of an offence under this section, the court that imposes the sentence shall consider as an aggravating factor the fact that the person committed the offence with intent to make a profit.

Defence (5) It is not a defence to a charge under subsection (2) in respect of a visual representation that the accused believed that a person shown in the representation that is alleged to constitute child pornography was or was depicted as being eighteen years of age or more unless the accused took all reasonable steps to ascertain the age of that person and took all reasonable steps to ensure that, where the person was eighteen years of age or more, the representation did not depict that person as being under the age of eighteen years.

Defence (6) No person shall be convicted of an offence under this section if the act that is alleged to constitute the offence

(a) has a legitimate purpose related to the administration of justice or to science, medicine, education or art; and

(b) does not pose an undue risk of harm to persons under the age of eighteen years.

> Question of law (7) For greater certainty, for the pur-
> poses of this section, it is a question of law whether
> any written material, visual representation or audio
> recording advocates or counsels sexual activity with a
> person under the age of eighteen years that would be
> an offence under this Act."

http://laws-lois.justice.gc.ca/eng/acts/C-46/section-163.1.htm

Age of Consent for Pornography in Canada

The age of consent for viewing pornography was raised from 14 to 16 years in Canada May 1, 2008.

http://www.justice.gc.ca/eng/rp-pr/other-autre/clp/faq.html

APPENDIX B ACRONYMS

Parents should be aware of these acronyms as part of their digital supervision of children and youth.

AFK / BAK

Away from keyboard/ Back at keyboard

121

One-to-one

ASL?

Age, sex, location?

PA/ PAL/ POS/ P911

Parent alert/Parents are listening/

Parents over shoulder/ Parent alert

NIFOC

Naked in front of computer

MorF

Male or female

SorG

Straight or gay

LMIRL

Let's meet in real life

TDTM

Talk dirty to me

ADR

Address

WYCM?

Will you call me?

F2F

Face to face

WRN?

What's your real name?

WUF?

Where are you from?

53x

Sex

Cyber

Cybersex, sex over the computer

WTGP

Want to go private?

APPENDIX C DEFINITIONS AND TERMINOLOGY

For reader understanding of the terminology in this book, the following definitions are provided. Definitions to these and others can be found easily online with a simple search such as "basic computer terms" or similar glossaries. I have provided a few to get you started.

FaceTime – Begun by Apple in 2010. This is used on iPads and iPhones. Users will contact someone through their iPad or iPhone and be able to engage in one-on-one video chats. This is problematic when children and youth decide to transmit nudes to the recipient user. Laptops with webcams are used for this purpose as well, but simply referred to as webcam video.

Free Private Chat Rooms – Users can sign up for private chats with one or more people. Children or teens in this type of environment should be monitored as to the people in the chats.

Free Video Chat Rooms – Users can have webcam videos exchanged through these rooms. Obviously, these types of chats need to be monitored.

Hackers – It is illegal to hack into a computer network, yet children and youth believe it to be "funny". They often try to do it just to prove they can. Parents need to discuss this type of activity with their children and explain the possible legal actions that can be taken against them if they do this. Activity can be traced. Ground rules should be made with children by the parent/caregiver to ensure that the child/youth does not put himself/herself in any type of comprising situation with law enforcement. Teens may hack into games when they are playing with other players.

Host – A computer or network connected to the Internet.

Identity Theft – This is becoming more common through the use of computers and other devices. Through online private chats with children and teens, criminals can obtain personal information about them or their parents that can be used for identity theft. Parents need to be vigilant with children to ensure that does not happen. The vulnerability and trust of the child is used.

Internet Protocol Address – Often referred to as the "IP" address. This is a unique number that is different for each computer. "Unique" should be interpreted the same way as a cell phone or phone number. No two households have the same phone number or individuals the same cell number, which is the same for computer IP addresses – they are not duplicated. When law enforcement is looking for a source device, the IP number is their main focus.

Modem or Router – Device for connecting a host to the Internet. This includes dial-up modems and routers that may use standard telephone lines and dedicated cable modems.

Online Sexual Exploitation – Victims can have a predator make demands for money. A victim could have exposed themselves and knowingly or unknowingly been recorded by a predator. They may threaten the victim that the pictures or videos will be shared with other friends on Facebook or other social media. Unfortunately, sometimes the recording was done without the victim's knowledge. A well-known victim of this type of extortion was Amanda Todd.

OS – The operating system of a computer. Windows is the main operating system for a PC; Yosemite is a possible OS for a Mac.

Peer-to-peer Networking - A network in which file sharing can be done without easy detection. This is commonly called P2P activity. All computers have to have a common file-sharing program in order to connect. (e.g. Torrent, KaZaA, Morpheus, LimeWire).

Phishing – The act of attempting to obtain personal data from users fake information and emails.

Public Chat Rooms – Forums where people can chat about a number of topics. For example, sports enthusiasts can enter a chat about their favourite sport.

Remote Access Tool (RAT) - allows an attacker to gain full control of a user's computer when installed. Microsoft Windows-based computers are the most susceptible to this malware.

Revenge Porn – Children and youth use this to exercise revenge against another child or youth. If they have pictures that can be humiliating or embarrassing, they will use the pictures in an act of vindictiveness such as a boyfriend's former girlfriend or a girlfriend who has turned into someone's enemy. Pictures can be sent to mutual friends or unknown individuals as a revenge technique.

Screen Capture - Copying what is currently displayed on a screen to a file or printer.

Self-exploitation – Children and youth creating, sending, possessing, or sharing videos/pictures using webcams, cell phones, iPads, messaging applications or other electronic cellular devices. To be self-exploited, these pictures would be of a personal nature.

Selfie – Using an electronic device (particularly cell phones) of people taking pictures of themselves.

Server – A computer configured to provide a service to enable communication between computers in a network, including access to software and central storage of files. Attached to a server can be an email server for certain businesses.

Sexting – Users use cell phones to text sexual comments or to send nudes of themselves to other users.

Spambot – A spambot is a program designed to e-mail addresses in order to build mailing lists for sending unsolicited e-mail, also known as spam. Spambots are sometimes programmed to go to special webcam shows, which can be sexual.

URL – Universal Resource Locater – Universal Resource Locator – A web page's unique location or address. The reason it is referred to as "universal" is because web pages will appear the same in any browser or computer operating system. E.g. a Windows OS using Internet Explorer will view the webpage the same as a Mac OS using Safari.

Example:

http://www.childpornographyhurts.com

User – any human being using a computer, cell phone, electronic cellular device, and the like.

Viewing Pornography – It is illegal for anyone under the age of 16 to view pornography in Canada. This law was changed in 2008. It used to be 14. This should be explained to your children.

Web Browser – Software that allows web pages to be accessed and viewed. This is often confused with a "search engine." A search engine would be Yahoo, Google, or others that provide an environment that enables searching the Internet for data. There are thousands of queries using search engines for abusive images daily.

Webcam Blackmail – A predator will groom and then lure victims into taking off their clothes, while secretly recording them using the webcam of the user. They are able to do it in secret because they are actually not speaking live to the user but using a video they have prerecorded so the victim believes the webcam is being used by the predator in real time. This recording will be unknown until the predator plays it for the user. The video is then used for blackmail of the victim. The blackmail could be for money, revenge, emotional abuse, etc.

YouTube – A popular video-sharing website.

CITATIONS

"Age of Consent to Sexual Activity." Government of Canada, Department of Justice, Electronic Communications. Web. 5 Nov. 2015.

"An Act Respecting the Mandatory Reporting of Internet Child Pornography by Persons Who Provide an Internet Service (S.C. 2011, C. 4)." Legislative Services Branch. Government of Canada, 23 Mar. 2011. Web. 4 Jan. 2016.

"Child Abuse and Neglect in Connecticut." Connecticut Judicial Branch Law Libraries. State of Connecticut, 2015. Web. Jan.-Feb. 2016.

"Child Pornography and Abuse Statistics - Thorn." Thorn. Wearethorn.org, 2016. Web. Apr.-May 2016.

"Child Pornography Laws in the United States." Wikipedia. Wikimedia Foundation. Web. Jan. 2016.

"Criminal Code (R.S.C., 1985, C. C-46)." Legislative Services Branch. Web. 2 Nov. 2015. Feb.-Mar. 2016.

"Critical Infrastructure Protection." Wikipedia. Wikimedia Foundation. Web. 2 Mar. 2016.

"Critical Infrastructure Protection." Wikipedia. Wikimedia Foundation. Web. 16 Mar. 2016.

"Critical Infrastructure." Critical Infrastructure. Public Safety Canada, Government of Canada. Web. 14 Mar. 2016.

"Dark Web." Wikipedia. Wikimedia Foundation. Web. 10 Jan. 2016.

"Digital Devices and Children." Parents.com. Parents. Web. Mar. 2016.

"Geotagging." Wikipedia. Wikimedia Foundation. Web. 2 Feb. 2016.

"History of the Internet." Wikipedia. Wikimedia Foundation. Web. 10 Jan. 2016.

"Humanity Dictionary Definition | Humanity Defined." Your Dictionary. Web. 1 May 2016.

"MS-DOS." Wikipedia. Wikimedia Foundation. Web. Jan.-Feb. 2016.

"NCA National Statistics Report." National Children's Alliance. NCA. Web. Mar.-Apr. 2016.

"Operation Avalanche (child Pornography Investigation)." Wikipedia. Wikimedia Foundation. Web. 7 Apr. 2016.

"Operation Candyman." FBI. FBI National Press Office, 18 Mar. 2002. Web. 21 Mar. 2016.

"Operation Cathedral." Wikipedia. Wikimedia Foundation. Web. 1 Feb. 2016.

"Pennsylvania Man Arrested for Child Pornography." ICE |. 2 Apr. 2015. Web. 6 Feb. 2016.

"Pornography Addiction." - Wikipedia, the Free Encyclopedia. Wikimedia Foundation. Web. 12 Apr. 2016.

"Proxy Server." Wikipedia. Wikimedia Foundation. Web. Jan.-Feb. 2016.

"Search Engine Indexing." Wikipedia. Wikimedia Foundation. Web. 10 Jan. 2016.

"Set up Parental Controls - Windows Help." Windows.microsoft.com. Microsoft. Web. Feb.-Mar. 2016.

"Sexting Acronyms." COMEC The Commission on Missing Exploited Children. Web. Jan.-Feb. 2016.

"Snapchat - App Review." Snapchat App Review. Commonsensemedia. org. Web. 6 Apr. 2016.

"Steve Jobs." Wikipedia. Wikimedia Foundation. Web. Jan.-Feb. 2016.

"Trace Email." Accurate Email Tracer. IP Address. Web. Mar.-Apr. 2016.

"Victims of Child Pornography." Improving the Response to. National Center For Victims Of Crime. Web. Jan. 2016.

Admin. "Erectile Dysfunction Increases among Young Men, Sex Therapist Brandy Engler, PhD." Your Brain On Porn. Your Brain On Porn, 25 July 2013, 22:12. Web. 17 Mar. 2016, 10:30 a.m.

Bogart, Nicole. "What You Need to Know about the BlackShades Malware." Global News What You Need to Know about the BlackShades Malware. Global News Toronto, 20 May 2014. Web. Jan.-Feb. 2016.

Bogart, Nicole. "What You Need to Know about Webcam Hacking and How to Prevent It." Global News Toronto, 11 Aug. 2015, 11:57 a.m.. Web. Jan.-Feb. 2016.

Boyce, Jillian. "Police-reported Crime Statistics in Canada, 2014." Government of Canada, Statistics Canada, 2014. Web. Jan.-Feb. 2016.

Brantford, News. "Teen Charged with Distributing Intimate Image." Brantford Expositor, News Brantford, Brant, 21 Jan. 2016. Web. 25 Jan. 2016.

Carey, Tanith. "Why More and More Women Are Using Pornography." The Guardian. Guardian News and Media, 07 Apr. 2011, 21:00,. Web. Apr. 2016.

Carn, Billie. "The Internet of Humanity [IoH]." The Huffington Post. TheHuffingtonPost.com, 4 May 2016, 3:24 p.m. ET. Web. 8 May 2016, 8:00 p.m.

Cooper, Roy. "Is Your Child At Risk Online?" Is Your Child At Risk Online? North Carolina Department of Justice. Web. 5 Feb. 2016.

FBI. "Overview and History of the Violent Crimes Against Children Program." FBI. FBI, 2010. Web. Jan.-Feb. 2016.

Finch, Samantha. "Online Sexual Predators Baiting Children Caught in Police Sting." Parent Herald RSS. Parent Herald, 10 Apr. 2016, 6:20 p.m. Web. 12 Apr. 2016.

Jack Doyle for the Daily Mail. "A Facebook Crime Every 40 Minutes: From Killings to Grooming as 12,300 Cases Are Linked to the Site." Mail Online. Associated Newspapers, 05 June 2012. Web. 21 Mar. 2016.

Jones, Lisa M., Kimberly J. Mitchell, and Heather A. Turner. "Victim Reports of Bystander Reactions to In-Person and Online Peer Harassment: A National Survey of Adolescents." University of New Hampshire, Education. Crossmark, 5 June 2015. Web. 5 Jan. 2016.

Kelion, Leo. "Microsoft Tip Leads to Child Porn Arrest in Pennsylvania." BBC News. 6 Aug. 2014. Web. 21 Mar. 2016.

Kelly, Amanda, "10 Laval Teens Face Child Pornogrpahy Charges; Girls Unaware Photos Shared". Global News Toronto, , 14 Nov. 2014. Web. 5 Mar. 2016.

King, Miriam. "Think, before You Hit Send." Bradford Times. Bradford Times.ca, 20 Mar. 2014., 4:28 EDT p.m, Web. Feb.-Mar. 2016.

Kristy. "Why Modern Parenting Is Hard." Every Chance To Learn. Every Chance To Learn, Nov. 2014. Web. 20 Dec. 2015.

Lewis, Marieke, Patrick Miller, and Alice R. Buchalter. "Internet Crimes Against Children: An Annotated Bibliography of Major Studies." Loc.Gov. Federal Research Division, Library of Congress, Washington, D.C., Oct. 2009. Web. Feb.-Mar. 2016.

Lieberman, Caryn, and Adam Miller. "Toronto Woman's Webcam Hacked While Watching Netflix." Global News Toronto Womans Webcam Hacked

While Watching Netflix. Global News Toronto, 10 Aug. 2015, 11:07 a.m. Web. 22 Jan. 2016.

M'Jid, Najat Maalia. "Child Pornography Flourishes in a World with No Borders." Child Pornography Flourishes in a World with No Borders. United Nations Human Rights, Office of the High Commissioner, 29 Nov. 2009. Web. 2 May 2016.

McRoberts, Meghan. "Sexting Acronyms Parents Need to Know." WPTV. 10 Dec. 2014. Web. 12 Mar. 2016.

Meissner, Dirk. "Sexting B.C. Teen Found Guilty of Child Pornography." British Columbia. The Canadian Press, 10 Jan. 2014. Web. 21 Feb. 2016.

Mesmer, Aaron. "Sheriff, School Take on Lake Placid Teen Sexting Scandal." WTVT. Fox 13, 18 Feb. 2016, 6:41 p.m. Web. 21 Feb. 2016, 11:15 a.m.

"Metadata." Wikipedia. Wikimedia Foundation. Web. Mar.-Apr. 2016.

Mick, Jason. "Unsecured Routers Land People in a Heap of Police Trouble -." Daily Tech. Daily Tech, 15 Apr. 2011. Web. 5 Jan. 2016.

Moran, Lee. "North Carolina Teens Arrested for Sending Nude Selfies, Videos to One Another: Cops." New York Daily News. 21 Sept. 2015. Web. 5 Mar. 2016.

NCJRS. "Internet Crimes Against Children." U.S. Department of Justice. NCJRS, Dec. 2001. Web. Feb.-Mar. 2016.

Ncmec. "The Real Story: Victim of Sexual Abuse Speaks out." Missing Kids. NCMEC, 2014. Web. Mar. 2016.

News, CBC. "Teens Charged with Distributing Child Porn Online in Kamloops - British Columbia - CBC News." CBCnews. CBC/Radio Canada, 13 Feb. 2014. Web. 2 Jan. 2016.

NoBullying, "Teen Sexting, Statistics and Consequences", Bullying CyberBullying Resources. NoBullying.com, 17 Dec. 2014. Web. Apr. 2016.

Persin, Coby. "The Dangers Of Social Media (Child Predator Social Experiment) Girl Edition!" YouTube. YouTube, 10 Aug. 2015. Web. 14 Apr. 2016.

"PhotoDNA." Wikipedia. Wikimedia Foundation. Web. Mar.-Apr. 2016.

"Police-reported Sexual Offences against Children and Youth in Canada, 2012." Government of Canada, Statistics Canada., 2014. Web. Jan.-Feb. 2016.

Pulido, Ph.D. Mary L. "Child Pornography: Basic Facts About a Horrific Crime." The Huffington Post. TheHuffingtonPost.com, 17 Oct. 2013, 12:54 p.m. Web. Jan.-Feb. 2016.

Pulido, Ph.D. Mary L. "Exploring Why Offenders View Internet Child Pornography." The Huffington Post. TheHuffingtonPost.com, 29 Feb. 2016. Web. Mar.-Apr. 2016.

Pulido, Ph.D. Mary L. "Fighting Internet Child Pornography." The Huffington Post. TheHuffingtonPost.com, 19 July 2014. Web. Jan.-Feb. 2016.

Rouse, Margaret. "What Is Spambot? - Definition from WhatIs.com." SearchExchange. WhatIs.com, 2003. Web. 25 Jan. 2016.

Ryan, Patty. "A Victim of Child Pornography Doesn't Get to Forget." Tampa Bay Times.13 Dec. 2013, 1:08 p.m., Web. 12 Feb. 2016, 12:15 p.m.

Sherwell, Philip. "US Investigators Arrest 14 'operators' of Massive Global Child Pornography Website." The Telegraph. Telegraph Media Group, 19 Mar. 2014. Web. Jan.-Feb. 2016.

Skelton, Alissa. "20 Infamous Crimes Committed and Solved on Facebook [INFOGRAPHIC]." Mashable. 01 Mar. 2012. Web. 21 Mar. 2016.

Staff, Webopedia. "Screen Capture." What Is ? Webopedia Definition. Webopedia. Web. 20 Mar. 2016.

Staff. "Ready For A Close-Up? Watch Out For Selfie Addiction! | Addiction. com." Addictioncom. Technology Addiction, 23 May 2014. Web. Feb.-Mar. 2016.

Steurer, Geoff. "How Pornography Affects Women and What They Can Do." S.A. Lifeline Foundation. Safeline.org. Web. 20 Apr. 2016.

Thomas, Emily. "Google Reports Man Allegedly Sending Child Porn In Email." The Huffington Post. TheHuffingtonPost.com, 4 Aug. 2014. Web. 6 Feb. 2016.

Tran, Mark. "Six Types of Killer Use Facebook to Commit Crimes, Says Study." The Guardian. Guardian News and Media, 03 Nov. 2014. Web. 10 Jan. 2016.

"Webopedia: Online Tech Dictionary for IT Professionals." Webopedia. Web. Feb.-Mar. 2016.

Wright, Michael P. "Ensis Wiki." - Pedophilia in Ancient Greece and Rome. Ensis Wiki. Web. 21 Mar. 2016.

Thank you for caring enough about
CHILD PROTECTION
to read this book. We need to practice
DIGITAL SUPERVISION
To protect ALL of OUR children.
Be on the safe side.
Communicate with your children.
Foster positive energy, positive behaviours,
positive futures.
Protect our most vulnerable sector – our children.
Our children are our future,
our leaders of tomorrow.
Practice DIGITAL SUPERVISION
Refuse to be a bystander to
DIGITAL VICTIMIZATION AND CRIME.

A portion of the proceeds of this book will be
donated to **Child Pornography Hurts**,

a Canadian charity dedicated to support-
ing victims and fighting the crime of

child pornography.

If you are interested in making a donation, please go to:

http://www.childpornographyhurts.com

We need funding to help victims.

Thank you

CPSIA information can be obtained
at www.ICGtesting.com
Printed in the USA
LVHW04s1025120518
576943LV00005B/16/P